HONOR'S REWARD

HONOR'S
REWARD

*How to Attract
God's Favor and Blessing*

JOHN BEVERE

NEW YORK   BOSTON   NASHVILLE

Unless otherwise indicated, Scriptures are taken from the NEW KING JAMES
    VERSION. Copyright © 1979, 1980, 1982, Thomas Nelson, Inc., Publishers.
Scriptures noted The Message are taken from The Message. Copyright © 1993, 1994, 1995,
    1996, 2000, 2001, 2002. Used by permission of NavPress Publishing Group.
Scriptures noted TEV are taken from TODAY'S ENGLISH VERSION. Copyright © American
    Bible Society 1966, 1971, 1976, 1992.
Scriptures noted NLT are taken from the *Holy Bible,* New Living Translation, copyright © 1996.
    Used by permission of Tyndale House Publishers, Inc., Wheaton, Illinois 60189. All rights
    reserved.
Scriptures noted AMP are taken from the Amplified® Bible. Copyright © 1954, 1962, 1965, 1987
    by The Lockman Foundation. Used by permission.
Scriptures noted CEV are taken from THE CONTEMPORARY VERSION. © 1991 by the
    American Bible Society. Used by permission.
Scriptures noted NASB are taken from the New American Standard Bible®. Copyright © 1960,
    1962, 1963, 1968, 1972, 1975, 1977, 1995 by The Lockman Foundation. Used by permission.
Scriptures noted NCV are taken from The Holy Bible, New Century Version®, copyright © 1987,
    1988, 1991 by Word Publishing, a division of Thomas Nelson, Inc. Used by permission.
Scriptures noted NIV are taken from the HOLY BIBLE: NEW INTERNATIONAL VER-
    SION®. Copyright © 1973, 1978, 1984 by International Bible Society. Used by permission of
    Zondervan Publishing House. All rights reserved.
Scriptures noted ASV are taken from the American Standard Version. Public domain.

FaithWords
Hachette Book Group USA
237 Park Avenue
New York, NY 10017

Visit our Web site at www.faithwords.com.

Printed in the United States of America

First Edition: November 2007
10 9 8 7 6 5 4 3 2

FaithWords is a division of Hachette Book Group USA, Inc.
The FaithWords name and logo is a trademark of Hachette Book Group USA, Inc.

Library of Congress Cataloging-in-Publication Data

Bevere, John.
    Honor's reward : how to attract God's favor and blessing / John Bevere. — 1st ed.
        p. cm.
    Summary: "In his life-changing new book, Honor's reward, bestselling author John Bevere explains
the paradox of how our greatest success comes from honoring others."—Provided by the publisher.
    ISBN-13: 978-0-446-57883-7
    ISBN-10: 0-446-57883-5
    1. Honor—Religious aspects—Christianity. 2. Respect—Religious aspects—Christianity.
3. Authority—Religious aspects—Christianity. 4. Success—Religious aspects—Christianity. I. Title.
    BV4647.H6B48 2007
    241'.4—dc22   2007010690

In honor of three important men in my life:

Jim Heeres

who introduced me to Jesus Christ

Mark Stoehr

who brought me to Jesus Christ

Don Blake

who established me in Jesus Christ

One sowed, one reaped, one trained, but God gave the increase.
To God be all the Glory!

CONTENTS

ACKNOWLEDGMENTS ix

CHAPTER 1 *Rewards Await You* 1

CHAPTER 2 *Partial and No Rewards* 11

CHAPTER 3 *Full Reward* 21

CHAPTER 4 *Little to Do with the Leader* 31

CHAPTER 5 *Authority* 41

CHAPTER 6 *Harsh Authority* 56

CHAPTER 7 *Honoring Civil Leaders* 67

CHAPTER 8 *Honoring Social Leaders* 83

CHAPTER 9 *Honoring Domestic Leaders* 93

CHAPTER 10 *Honoring Church Leaders* 110

CHAPTER 11 *Double Honor* 127

CHAPTER 12 *Honoring Our Peers* 147

CHAPTER 13 *Honoring Those Entrusted to Us* 161

CHAPTER 14 *Honor in the Home—Children* 175

CHAPTER 15 *Honor in the Home—Wife* 187

CHAPTER 16 *Honor All* 201

CHAPTER 17 *Honoring God* 209

ACKNOWLEDGMENTS

My deepest appreciation to . . .

Lisa. Thanks for being my wife, best friend, most faithful supporter, co-laborer in the ministry, mother of our children, and lover. You are truly God's gift to me, and I value and treasure you. I love you, babe.

Our four sons, Addison, Austin, Alexander, and Arden. All of you have brought great joy to my life. You are each a special treasure to me. Thank you for sharing in the call of God and encouraging me to travel and write. I love spending time with each of you.

The staff and board members of Messenger International. Thank you for your unwavering support and faithfulness. It's a pleasure to work with each of you and an honor to serve God together. Lisa and I love each of you.

Our many ministerial friends all over the world. Space doesn't permit me to write each of your names. Thanks for the invitations and honor to speak and minister in your churches and conferences. I love all you pastors and ministers who are serving God faithfully.

Acknowledgments

Tom Winters and Rolf Zetterson, thanks for your encouragement and belief in the message God has burned in my heart.

Gary Terashita, thank you for your editing skills in this project. But most of all thanks for your support.

All the staff of FaithWords. Thanks for the support of this message and for your professional and kind help. You are a great group to work with.

Most important, my sincere gratitude to my Lord. How can words adequately acknowledge all You have done for me and for Your people? I love You more than I am able to express.

HONOR'S REWARD

CHAPTER 1

Rewards Await You

૪

Honor. Though it is almost an extinct virtue in the twenty-first century, the concept still holds the power to move us. In movies a display of honor can inspire tears as courage and sacrifice are witnessed. Review the greatest blockbusters of all time and you'll find honor interwoven into their plots. We applaud its virtue vicariously, but where is honor in our everyday lives? The notion that it could be lived in the ordinary has become foreign to our generation.

I want to see honor restored to the sons and daughters of God. It is the essential key to receiving from God, and for this very reason the enemy of our souls has all but eliminated the true power of honor. Honor carries with it great rewards; rewards God desires you to have. Honor has the power to greatly enhance your life.

You are about to embark on a journey that will take you closer to the heart of God, the author of all that is honorable. I pray these revelatory truths will affect your life in a profound and practical way. Many have not learned these lessons until much later in life. For this reason John the apostle urgently writes,

> "Look to yourselves, that we do not lose those things we worked for, but that we may receive a full reward."
>
> —2 John 8

John was an old man looking back over nearly a century of living when he penned those words (*Clarke's Commentary*, Abingdon Press (1977)—Accordance 6.6). He lent his hard-won insight for our benefit today. John had the acquired vantage realized by men and women who have lived long and well. It is a destination arrived at by faithfully walking in a life calling, a post of assurance and strength, something I call a *Grandfather* or *Grandmother Anointing*; and when they speak, the wise listen.

Over the past twenty-five years I've enjoyed a handful of encounters with such men and women. These are ambassadors who've worn life well and entered the stage where they look back with knowing. Such seasoned veterans develop some common attributes, three of which we will discuss here. First, they instinctively locate the heart of a matter. They don't beat around the bush, or waste time with the unimportant. Second, they say much in very few words. Third, the words they choose and utter are weighty. Their somewhat sparse communication carries a greater weight than the same words spoken by another who has not walked as well, or as long, the paths of life. After such an interlude I have found myself meditating for months on just one or two sentences uttered by these seasoned veterans.

In light of this reasoning we can assume John the apostle was saying a great deal. In fact, I've meditated on these inspired words for years, and the revelation within them continues to expand. Let's examine his admonishment a phrase at a time.

Don't Lose Your Inheritance

He begins, "Look to yourselves." John encourages each of us to *take heed, examine, and watch out for ourselves*. An urgency is lent to his words, for what he's about to communicate is not to be taken lightly, but thoroughly pondered.

Careful attention must be paid so we do not lose those things for which we have labored. This is a bit sobering . . . we can lose what was won through labor. Imagine a farmer toiling to clear his field. He works through the heat of the day to rid the soil of boulders and stumps that would hinder the soil from producing a harvest. Once cleared, he plows and tills the ground in preparation for the planting of his seed. Once the field is planted, he labors to maintain the ideal conditions for his plantings to flourish by fertilizing, weeding, and watering his seed. The plants emerge and his labor continues as he protects the field from pestilence and damage. Then a few weeks prior to harvest he is weary and gives up. All is for naught as he loses his entire crop because of his latter neglect. Or perhaps a storm threatened, he saw the warnings but neglected to respond, and the mistake cost him the ingathering. What a waste of time, money, labor, and resources only to falter at the moment of realization.

What about a businessman who labors to build his company for years, only to lose it in the end because of a few bad decisions? Again . . . tragic. In both cases the benefits of extensive labor are lost in a moment through wrong choices.

This is why Scripture repeatedly encourages us to finish well: "He who *endures to the end*" (Matt. 10:22; 24:13; Mark 13:13), again, "We have become partakers of Christ if we hold the beginning of our confidence steadfast *to the end*" (Heb. 3:14), and again, "He who overcomes, and keeps My works *until the end*" (Rev. 2:26, emphasis mine in all), and the list continues. Christianity is not a sprint but an endurance run. Therefore it is not how we start the race that counts, but how we complete it. How we finish is determined by the choices we make, and those are often formed by patterns we develop along the way.

Life-Defining Moments

There was an incident with one of our sons. He wanted to do something I wasn't in favor of. He knew where I stood yet I felt he was old enough to make the call, so the final decision was his.

Time passed and I found out he chose to go against my counsel. Later we sat down to discuss his choice. I explained, "The choice was up to you, but I want to take this opportunity to teach you from this.

"There was a young king named Rehoboam. Shortly after he began his reign a question arose from his subjects: 'Your father made our lives rough from the demands he placed upon us. Would you please lighten the load and we will happily serve you.'

"The young king instructed the people to return in a few days to hear his decision. His father's counselors told him, 'If you will be a servant to this people, be considerate of their needs and respond with compassion, work things out with them, they'll end up doing anything for you' [1 Kings 12:7, The Message].

"It was good and wise counsel, but the young king rejected their advice and went to his peers. They said, 'These people who complain, "Your father was too hard on us; lighten up"—well, tell them this: "My little finger is thicker than my father's waist. If you think life under my father was hard, you haven't seen the half of it. My father thrashed you with whips; I'll beat you bloody with chains!"' [vv. 10–11, The Message].

"The young king, Rehoboam, heeded his friends' advice with some tragic results. The kingdom his father Solomon built was torn, and ten out of the twelve tribes of Israel were permanently fragmented as five-sixths of the kingdom was torn from his iron fist. One bad choice cost him dearly for the rest of his life."

I then told my son, "Let's go back. Perhaps for years Prince Rehoboam and his friends spurned the counsel of his father Solomon, or his elders. Maybe they snickered over goblets of wine and shook their heads in the secrecy of the royal chambers at what they presumed to be foolish and old-fashioned advice. Vain thoughts may have cluttered Rehoboam's head: *I will keep my peace while I am yet a prince, but when I become king I will not listen to these silly old men.* As a prince his decisions to ignore and lightly esteem his elders' wisdom cost him very little. He did not realize the die had been set and one day he would be foolish while thinking himself wise. When his *life-defining moment* arose, he lacked the pattern necessary to execute sound judgment."

I continued: "We all have *life-defining moments*. They are like open-book tests, but we don't know we have been examined until it is over. Son, you decided not to heed my counsel and this time it cost you nothing. But the day will come when a *life-defining moment* arises. If you've already developed the pattern of heeding wise counsel, you will naturally follow suit and find yourself greatly rewarded."

Moving on from my son, let's review another example. The children of Israel had not developed a pattern of heeding God's word. He delivered them from bondage, but they repeatedly complained and disobeyed. There were times this behavior seemed to exact a minimum cost, and other times when it didn't appear to affect them at all. However, in the process a pattern was being established. Eventually their *life-defining moment* arose. Twelve spies were sent into Canaan to check out the land, which God set apart as theirs. The spies returned with a whiny, negative report, and the whole assembly followed and began to complain as before, but this time it cost them dearly. They would never enter the Promised Land and for the rest of their lives they would wander. In a moment's time they lost all they'd labored to possess. There was no reversal of their loss. Though they could see it they would never lay hold of it, just as Rehoboam lost the ten tribes for the rest of his life and generations afterward.

There is an important lesson for the young and old in this: we don't want to merely obey God; we need to catch His heart. It is then we will glimpse the wisdom behind His directives, and not just see them as laws. The young prince Rehoboam never caught his father's or his elders' hearts. The older generation of Israelites never quite saw what God was doing or the goodness of His heart toward them, and they lost everything.

Now let's look at the other side of the coin. There are examples throughout the Scriptures where individuals glimpsed God's heart and developed wise decision-making models. When those undetected *life-defining moments* occurred, they responded correctly and received great rewards.

The most simple way to not lose what we've labored for is to develop patterns of consistently honoring God's counsel. Each and every day we are presented with opportunities to make choices. The day will come when we will look back and know which were in fact *life-defining*, but if we've developed godly patterns we'll continue to follow suit, and later realize our reward.

Rewards

This brings us to John's next point; and for ease of reference we'll review the entire verse: "Look to yourselves, that we do not lose those things we worked for, *but that we may receive a full reward*." Note God is a *Rewarder* (see Heb. 11:6). This is a truth we must establish deep within our hearts. In fact, He loves to reward. How did He introduce Himself to Abraham? "After these things the word of the LORD came to Abram in a vision, saying, 'Do not be afraid, Abram. I am your shield, *your exceedingly great reward*'" (Gen. 15:1, emphasis mine).

He said, "I am your . . . *exceedingly great reward*." Wow, what a way to present yourself. Psalm 19:9–11 echoes this: "The ordinances of the Lord are true and righteous altogether . . . *in keeping them there is great reward*" (AMP, emphasis mine). We read in Psalm 57:2, "I will cry to God Most High, Who performs on my behalf and *rewards me* [Who brings to pass His purposes for me and surely completes them]!" (AMP, emphasis mine).

God is a Rewarder and loves to reward His children! As a father of four sons I've discovered a portion of this delight. I love to see their eyes light up with gratefulness, and watch fulfillment settle upon them as they bask in the afterglow of a choice made well and rewarded. However, I've also learned it is unwise to reward bad behavior. By rewarding those who don't deserve it or have not earned it, you destroy the power of incentive; and incentive is a good thing. My boys know I love them, but over the years they've grown to understand the difference between my love and pleasure. God loves each of us deeply, and His love is perfect. However, that doesn't necessarily mean there won't be times when He's altogether pleased with our actions or choices. God rewards those He is pleased with, which are those who heed His counsel.

Notice John says, "That we may receive a *full* reward." While I meditated, the word *full* jumped off the page. I thought, *If there's a full reward, then there's a partial reward, and even a no-reward scenario.* (Remember, we are not talking salvation here, but rewards.) Upon further meditation I concluded there are two applications to which John is referring. The first is the Judgment Seat of Christ. Paul states: "We are confident, yes, well pleased rather to be absent from the body and to be present with the Lord" (2 Cor. 5:8).

We know immediately Paul is not addressing all humanity, for when an unbeliever is absent from the body he is not present with the Lord; rather he is in hell. This may sound harsh, but it's the truth. Jesus didn't come into our world to condemn it, quite the contrary, to save it. The world was already condemned because of Adam, who sold us over to eternal death (see John 3:17–18). Only those who receive Jesus the Christ by committing their lives completely to Him will be present with the Lord when they leave behind their earthly bodies. Paul continues to address the believers:

> Therefore we make it our aim, whether present or absent,
> to be well pleasing to Him. For we must all appear before

the judgment seat of Christ, that each one may receive the things done in the body, according to what he has done, whether good or bad.

—2 Corinthians 5:9–10

Every believer will stand before Christ's Judgment Seat. On that day each of us will receive according to what we did in our short time on earth. The Today's English Version states, "We will each receive what we deserve." Our sins will not be judged, for the blood of Jesus eradicated the eternal punishment ascribed to sin. Rather, we will be rewarded, or suffer loss, for what we did as believers. Our deeds, words, thoughts, and even motives will be inspected in the light of His Word. The temporary things on which we built our lives will be devoured, which will result in loss, and the eternal will be purified into everlasting rewards (see 1 Cor. 3:14–15).

The scope of loss suffered to rewards will vary from having everything we did consumed, yet we'll be saved, but as through fire; all the way to the heights of reigning alongside Jesus Christ forever and ever (see 1 Cor. 3:15; Rev. 3:21). This is certainly a vast range. The first would be our example of a "no-reward" situation; the latter would be an example of the "full-reward" scenario, with the partial reward falling anywhere in between.

These Judgment Seat decisions are called "eternal judgments" (see Heb. 6:1–2), which means there will never be any alterations, amendments, or changes made to those decrees. Therefore, it can be concluded that what we do with the cross of Christ determines *where* we'll spend eternity; however, the way we live thereafter as believers determines *how* we'll spend it.

It is wise therefore to look diligently into what Scripture says about eternal judgments and rewards. This knowledge is described as an elementary teaching of Christ. In elementary school, your foundation is laid with all your educational building blocks, such as reading, writing, math, etc. Can you imagine trying to build your high school or college education without knowing how to read, write, add, or subtract? It would be impossible. Yet far too many believers attempt to build their Christian lives without this elementary knowledge of the teaching of Christ. The urgency of this dilemma moved me to write *Driven by Eternity*, which addresses this issue in detail, and I recommend it as a companion to this message.

This Life

We've established that godly patterns carry the promise of reward at the Judgment Seat, but their blessing reaches us in this life as well. We read, "Godliness is profitable for all things, having promise of the life that *now is* and of *that which is to come*" (1 Tim. 4:8, emphasis mine).

Our Father desires to reward us both then and now as we heed His counsel. We are told, "The righteous will be rewarded in the earth" (Prov. 11:31, NASB). Not just in heaven, but in this life. And again, "Righteous people will be rewarded with good things" (Prov. 13:21, TEV). James is emphatic when he states, "Do not be deceived, my beloved brethren. Every good gift and every perfect gift is from above, and comes down from the Father" (James 1:16–17).

Good is from God. Don't ascribe the harmful and detrimental to God; He is the giver of good. God's desire is to reward you with His benefits here and now. His rewards carry no backlash with them. We are told, "The blessing of the LORD makes one rich, and he adds no sorrow with it" (Prov. 10:22). And again, "The trustworthy will get a rich reward" (Prov. 28:20, NLT). The *rich reward* is the *full reward*.

Continuing to ponder the apostle John's words, I thought, *For there to be full-, partial-, and no-reward scenarios in our future, then it stands to reason that, too, would apply to this present life.* Upon reviewing the life of Jesus this became evident. As He walked this earth encountering mankind, there were some who received the partial reward, others who received nothing, and those who attained full-portion rewards. Let's look at a sampling of each, and watch for the patterns that emerge, which will show us the way He desires for each of us.

CHAPTER 2

Partial and No Rewards

❧

Nazareth anxiously anticipated the promised manifestation of Messiah; they were watchfully aware because it was the season He was to appear. They were not unlike Christians in our day, for most know we are in the period preceding His second coming. Jesus said we would know the season or generation, but not the day or hour. So there is no reason to think it odd the Israelites knew the season of His first coming. Daniel gave the time frame in his writings (Dan. 9:24–26), and the experts in the law told the wise men where to find the child Jesus (see Matt. 2:4). They knew the time was upon them, but once the Messiah was revealed in their midst we find a puzzling reaction:

> "Now He *could do no* mighty work there, except that He laid His hands on a few sick people and healed them."
>
> —Mark 6:5 (emphasis mine)

Notice the words "*could do no* mighty work there." A few years ago while reading this scripture I was startled by this phrase. I thought, *Wait a minute, it doesn't say, "He would do no mighty work," but rather it specifies, "He could do no mighty work there."* Had it said the former, I

11

wouldn't have given it a second thought, because it would deal with Jesus' will. However, "could do no" meant He wasn't withholding; rather He was restrained. This point is emphasized and clarified in other translations as well; the Amplified Bible says, "He was not able to do."

Our question becomes, Why couldn't Jesus do any mighty works in Nazareth? What restrained Him? He performed great miracles in the other cities; the blind saw, deaf ears were opened, the crippled were suddenly walking, the dead raised. And this is just a sample of what was recorded. Frequently it was reported in the Gospels that He healed all manner of sickness and disease. What was the difference? Why were only a few sick healed in this city? Our answer is found in the words of the Nazarene people from the preceding verses:

> "Where did this man get these things? And what wisdom is this which is given to Him, that such mighty works are performed by His hands! Is this not the carpenter, the Son of Mary, and brother of James, Joses, Judas, and Simon? And are not His sisters here with us?" So they were offended at Him. But Jesus said to them, "A prophet is not without *honor* except in his own country, among his own relatives and in his own house."
>
> —Mark 6:2–4 (emphasis mine)

What's happening? Let's look. Jesus returned to the city He grew up in and joined God's people as they gathered on the Sabbath. The entire community is in the synagogue. When suddenly Jesus stands up and reads the following passage: "The Spirit of the LORD is upon Me, because He has anointed Me" (Luke 4:18).

The crowd knew what was coming—these were familiar words. They'd heard this passage in Isaiah numerous times; it was one of the main prophetic books that spoke of the coming Messiah. It would be no different than if today someone stood up and read the Beatitudes or the Lord's Prayer; we'd know what was coming next.

Jesus continued, "To preach the gospel to the poor . . . to heal the brokenhearted, to proclaim liberty to the captives and recovery of sight to the blind, to set at liberty those who are oppressed; to proclaim the acceptable year of the LORD" (vv. 18–20).

To this point there was only one point that needed to be addressed in these citizens' minds: why was this untrained young local reading the script rather than their seasoned rabbi? But suddenly the bomb is dropped; as Jesus rolls up the scroll He announces, "Today this Scripture is fulfilled in your hearing" (v. 21), then goes on to tell of the great and mighty works wrought in the other cities; and closes with a strong prophetic message.

What? Is He for real? Are they hearing correctly? Did He actually say He is the One about whom Isaiah prophesied? How preposterous! Insane! In utter disbelief the people begin to talk amongst themselves. "This is Jesus! What in the world is He doing? What is He saying?"

I can imagine one mother saying, "This can't be! He was in my son's Torah class!"

Stunned, another adds, "His family lives next door. He played with Benjamin!"

Others might have had more current memories: "He built the table we eat on every night! He built our chairs! He's the carpenter's son. What does He mean, 'The Spirit of the Lord is upon Me,' who does He think He is?"

Today we might protest, "He played soccer with my son!" or "He was in my daughter's math class!"

They formed a mental image of how their Messiah would come from their understanding of Old Testament scripture. Here's another familiar passage from Isaiah:

For unto us a Child is born, unto us a Son is given; and the government will be upon His shoulder. . . . Of the increase of His government and peace there will be no end, upon the throne of David and over His kingdom . . . from that time forward, even forever.

—Isaiah 9:6–7

These citizens were watching for a great King, One who would be both supernaturally wise and a powerful conqueror. He would swiftly deliver them from Roman oppression, and establish them as a nation without equal. He would regain the throne of David, and reign forever and ever. But when Jesus came as one of their own, raised in their schools, laughing in their streets, building household furniture, and surrounded by mafia (tax collectors) and prostitutes, they were blindsided. They couldn't grasp it. "Wait a minute," they cried within and without, "this is not the way we expected the Messiah to come!"

These local townspeople didn't realize there would be a few thousand years between the statement "a Son is given" and the total realization and physical manifestation, "of the increase of His government and peace there will be no end."

This incident, along with others like it throughout the Scriptures, reveals a truth that is hard to grasp: *often God will send us what we need in a package we don't want.* Why? To let us know He's God and we cannot second-guess Him. We cannot search for answers merely with our heads; we must seek Him and His provision with our hearts. Scripture cannot be interpreted from our limited human mental understanding. There must be a breath of the Spirit of God. He alone gives wise counsel and correct application.

A Stark Contrast

Allow me to give another example of this. The Pharisees were watching for a mighty conquering Messiah as well, a hero who would deliver God's people from Roman oppression. These leaders anxiously awaited His coming, believing they would be made under-rulers of this new kingdom established in Jerusalem. So when Jesus came on the scene as an untrained man from Galilee, they mocked Him. He didn't fit the image of their Messiah either.

In one of their many interrogations of Jesus, it is recorded, "Now when He was asked by the Pharisees when the kingdom of God would come, He answered them and said, 'The kingdom of God does not come with observation; nor will they say, "See here!" or "See there!" For indeed, the kingdom of God is within you'" (Luke 17:20–21).

Again these Pharisees were referring to Isaiah's prophecy of the Messiah's earthly kingdom. They, too, were looking for a Messiah based on their mental interpretation of scripture, rather than relying on the Spirit of God's leading. They knew God not by their hearts, but by their own reasoning.

In contrast, let's look at another man who was also watching for the Messiah. His name is Simeon. The Gospel of Luke tells us he was:

> just and devout, waiting for the Consolation of Israel, and the *Holy Spirit* was upon him. And it had been revealed to him by *the Holy Spirit* that he would not see death before he had seen the Lord's Christ. So he came *by the Spirit* into the temple. And when the parents brought in the Child Jesus, to do for Him according to the custom of the law he took Him up in his arms and blessed God and said . . .
>
> —Luke 2:25–28 (emphasis mine)

The summation of what Simeon spoke over Jesus was a declaration of this thirty-day-old baby as the Messiah. Now this is most interesting. Here is a man who recognizes the Messiah when He is but a month old, and yet all of Nazareth cannot recognize Him and the Pharisees mock Him when He is thirtysomething years of age, and performing signs and wonders no human being ever accomplished! Why? Again it is because God is Spirit, and those who would know Him and His ways must know Him by His Spirit who reveals truth. There is a key difference between Simeon and the others; and this truth we are about to see. This revelation will bring understanding to why so many do not receive their full inheritance from God.

Honor

To begin, let's again look at the statement Jesus made concerning His hometown's response to His ministry. He said, "A prophet is not without *honor* except in his own country, among his own relatives, and in his own house" (Mark 6:4, emphasis mine).

The key word here is *honor*. They didn't honor Him.

The Greek word for honor is *time* (pronounced "tee-mee"). I've done much study of this word, and the words closely related to it. I've looked in numerous Greek dictionaries, commentaries, and other books containing studies of the original Greek. I've also had in-depth talks with two fluent-speaking Greek men; one lives in Greece, his family is now four generations of ministers, the other, a minister living in Great Britian. The definitions I'm about to give are a combination of all the feedback I've received from these sources.

The simplistic and literal definition of *time* (honor) is "a valuing." When you speak of the word *time* to a Greek man, he thinks of something *valuable, precious, weighty,* such as gold. Think of it—you don't put gold in your junk drawer; rather you assign it a place of honor. Other definitions of honor are *appreciation, esteem, favorable regard, respect.*

Sometimes to better understand a word, look at its counterpart. The antonym of honor is *dishonor.* The Greek word is *atimia.* Some of its definitions are: *to not show respect or value; to treat as common, ordinary, or menial.* When you speak of dishonor to a Greek man, he would think of something *common, light, and easily done away with, such as vapor.* A stronger form of dishonor is to be treated shamefully and even humiliated.

From looking at my study of Greek dictionaries and commentaries I've discovered that honor can be displayed in action, word, and even thought. But all true honor originates from the heart. This is why God says, "Inasmuch as these people draw near with their mouths *and honor Me with their lips,* but have *removed their hearts far from Me,* and their *fear toward Me* is taught by the commandment of men" (Isa. 29:13, emphasis mine).

Notice God says, "their fear toward Me." True honor is an outflow from a heart that fears God. This is important, and we will discuss it further in a later chapter.

Jesus said these people of Nazareth withheld honor from Him. These hometown folks didn't treat Him as valuable and precious. They didn't recognize Him as One divinely sent to them to fulfill God's will. Rather they saw an ordinary man, a common local boy, standing before them. Because of this they only received a partial reward. Jesus was restrained from doing any mighty works. There was nothing notable that occurred; probably a few headaches, maybe arthritis or a couple bad backs were healed.

Think of it. Jesus—the Son of God, the Son of Man filled with God's Spirit without measure—is sent to heal the sick and all who were oppressed of the devil; but He cannot fulfill this commission, not because it wasn't God's will for all to be healed in that city, but because they restricted Him by withholding honor. They treated Him as a common local. Therefore they received a very small partial reward (just a few of the sick were healed).

A No-Reward Situation

In the Gospels we find another incident where Jesus is in a house teaching a multitude of teachers and experts of the Scriptures. These ministers came out of every town in Galilee and Judea to hear Him. We read: "And the power of the Lord was present to heal *them*" (Luke 5:17, emphasis mine).

Notice the word *them*—this would definitely refer to those in attendance. Now let me make a statement of truth: God never wastes anything. Oh yes, consider the time Jesus fed the four thousand and again the five thousand. In both cases He gave strict instructions to gather all the leftovers up so none would be lost. What many of us would have thrown away or dumped into the garbage disposal, He collected. You can see this same pattern throughout *all of Scripture in God's ways.* He never wastes anything.

So if the power of the Lord was present to heal the Pharisees and teachers of the law, that means there was at least one of *them*, and more than likely several who needed to be healed. In this, I speak from experience. Let's bring it forward to the present. Gather a few hundred people in a room, and with a group that large there are at least a dozen, and many times more, who have some kind of ailment. God's power is there to heal them all, but not one of them is healed.

Later, some men brought their paralyzed friend on a stretcher. After failing to gain entrance by the front door because the building was jammed full, they tried another route. Rather than give up, they went onto the housetop, tore open the tile roof, and let the paralytic down into the midst to Jesus. We then read: "When He saw their faith, He said to him, 'Man, your sins are forgiven you.' And the scribes and the Pharisees began to reason, saying, 'Who is this who speaks blasphemies? Who can forgive sins but God alone?'" (vv. 20–21).

Notice Luke writes the Pharisees, "began to reason, saying." Let's probe a little deeper. Did these leaders whisper to their comrades sitting nearest to them? Did they congregate in small groups and discuss Jesus' statement with one another? To bring clarity we need to go to Matthew's account. He writes they "said *within themselves*" (9:3, emphasis mine). So we see these teachers dishonored Jesus only with their thoughts. They spoke within themselves. They didn't speak aloud shameful, critical, or degrading words, but rather they were contrary only in thought. Mark writes as well that they were *"reasoning in their hearts"* (2:6). Listen to Jesus' response to their thoughts:

> But immediately, when Jesus perceived in His spirit that they reasoned thus within themselves, He said to them, "Why do you reason about these things in your hearts? Which is easier, to say to the paralytic, 'Your sins are forgiven you,' or to say, 'Arise, take up your bed and walk'? But that you may know that the Son of Man has power on earth to forgive sins"—He said to the paralytic, "I say to you, arise, take up your bed, and go to your house."
>
> —Mark 2:8–11

Immediately the paralytic rose up, picked up his bed, and walked out of the building in full sight of all the ministers. The Bible records that these preachers and teachers, "all were amazed and glorified God, saying, 'We never saw anything like this!' " (v. 12).

They were all amazed, but none of them was healed! They *received no reward* because they *dishonored* Jesus merely by way of thought! In this incident it wasn't their actions, nor their words, but their unvoiced thoughts. Remember, honor or dishonor can be displayed in deed, word, or thought, but all true honor originates from the heart.

Many of these Pharisees, teachers of the law, and scribes had already developed a pattern of dishonoring Jesus. They had mocked and disdained Him, and many times attempted to publicly shame Him. It is recorded, "So the scribes and Pharisees watched Him closely . . . that they might find an accusation against Him" (Luke 6:7). And again we read, "So they watched Him, and sent spies who pretended to be righteous, that they might seize on His words" (20:20). These are only a few accounts of many. As you can see, these men went beyond withholding honor to the place of dishonoring Jesus.

The people of Nazareth withheld honor, and received a small or *partial reward*. The Pharisees dishonored Jesus in thought and received *no reward*. Now let's examine those who received *full rewards* and see if there is any connection with the principle of honor.

CHAPTER 3

Full Reward

∞

Early in His ministry Jesus entered Capernaum and immediately encountered a Roman officer, a centurion in fact, who pleaded with Him to heal his paralyzed servant, who was dreadfully tormented. Jesus agreed, "I will come and heal him" (Matt. 8:7).

The centurion responded, "Lord, *I am not worthy* that You should come under my roof" (v. 8, emphasis mine).

Hold on, "not worthy"? This is the *conqueror* speaking to one of the *conquered*! Rome now occupied the nation of Israel. So why would this Roman officer tell a Jewish carpenter, "I'm not worthy for You to enter my home"? This would be like a colonel in the United States Marines telling an Iraqi plumber, "I'm not worthy to come to your house." Do you see how this man honors Jesus? See, the Roman officer knows who this carpenter really is. He treats Jesus as very important and renders due respect. The warrior goes on to explain, "But only speak a word, and my servant will be healed. *For I also* am a man under authority, having soldiers under me. And I say to this one, 'Go,' and he goes; and to another, 'Come,' and he comes; and to my servant, 'Do this,' and he does it" (vv. 8–9).

First let's discuss this officer's position or rank. There were six thousand soldiers in a Roman legion and one commander over that entire legion. Within the legion of six thousand there were sixty centurions who reported to the commander, and each centurion had one hundred soldiers under him.

He is explaining to Jesus how and why what he'd asked would work. He had the respect and obedience of his soldiers because he honored his commanding officer by submitting to his authority. He enjoyed the backing of his superior officer, who, in turn, was backed by the authority of Rome. To simplify we could say, "I have *authority because* I honor my country and my superiors by respecting their authority. So all I have to do is speak a word and those under me respond immediately to my directives."

Notice his preface, "For I *also.*" He recognized the authority of God on Jesus, therefore this officer knew Jesus exercised authority in the unseen spiritual realm, just as he wielded authority in the military world. This is why he understood all that was necessary was a simple command, and the infirmity would have to obey. In his mind it was no different than how those under his authority responded quickly to his orders. Look at Jesus' response:

> "When Jesus heard it, He marveled, and said to those who followed, 'Assuredly, I say to you, I have not found such great faith, not even in Israel!'"

—v. 10

Do you see this? Jesus announces this Roman officer had more faith than John the Baptist! Think of it. John the Baptist was of the house of Israel. Let's take this further; this officer had more faith than Jesus' mother Mary. Jesus declared his faith the greatest He'd encountered during his over thirty years in Israel . . . and Jesus never exaggerated. A Roman citizen and officer of the armed forces now occupying Israel wins the prize.

I'm a person of faith, and I hope you are too, because without faith it is impossible to please God (see Heb. 11:6). As Scripture records, "Faith comes by hearing, and hearing by the word of God" (Rom. 10:17). I would be willing to bet that John the Baptist heard far more scriptures than this Roman officer, yet this officer had more faith. I would also guess (and most likely be correct) that Mary, the mother of Jesus, the twelve disciples, and the many others in Israel whom Jesus encountered also had heard far more of the Word of God than this Roman officer, yet he had more faith than any of them. What made this faith of his so great? It was the coupling of the honor he showed Jesus and his understanding of authority. (Luke 17:5–10 shows it is not just hearing the Word of God that produces faith, but it must be supplemented with honor and compliance with authority.)

This man received his *full reward* because he rendered honor and understood authority. His regard for authority revealed a foundation of respect in his heart. So the root of his motivation was honor.

A Woman Who Would Not Be Denied

In the seventh chapter of Mark's Gospel we find a Greek woman, Syro-Phoenician by birth, coming to Jesus for help. The Scriptures state she kept asking Him to deliver her daughter from a demon. This infers that Jesus was not receptive to her first request, or second, and possibly multiple other petitions. It is quite probable He wouldn't even look at her. But she continued to ask. She is undaunted, and finally gets a response: "But Jesus said to her, 'Let the children be filled first, for it is not good to take the children's bread and throw it to the little dogs' " (v. 27).

Okay, you can slice the pie however you'd like, but it is coming out the same . . . Jesus called her a dog! I'm glad this woman wasn't an American. If so, Jesus might have gotten an earful. She might have lashed out, "What! Are You calling me a dog? What kind of minister are You? How dare You insult me in this way. I came for help, and this is the treatment I get? This is a racial thing . . . isn't it? Because I'm a Greek and You're a Jew, You think You have the right to call me a dog! This is an outrage. You sit there with Your staff and ignore a needy woman who's crying out for her daughter. Where is this love You preach about? Oh, I get it, there is no multitude to impress right now, just You and Your staff, so Your true colors are showing. You hypocrite, I've had enough . . . I'm out of here."

She would've stormed out and her daughter would not have been healed. She would have left with no reward. However, this woman did not behave in this manner. Instead she responded to His inference, and positioned herself for a reward: " 'Yes, Lord, yet even the little dogs under the table eat from the children's crumbs.' Then He said to her, 'For this saying go your way; the demon has gone out of your daughter' " (vv. 28–29).

I can almost see Jesus smile and shake His head as He admired the faith of this Gentile woman. How can she be denied? He tells her the demon that had tormented her daughter is gone, and the mother goes home to find her daughter free!

If she had been passive, or easily offended, she would have lost any hope of reward. She knew who Jesus was and persistently honored Him, first by her tenacity and then by not reviling or quitting even when it appeared she was insulted or dishonored. For her determination, she received a *full reward*.

It's interesting to note that both of these examples of amazing faith were Gentiles, those who walked outside the covenant of Abraham. A centurion and Greek woman caused Jesus to marvel at their faith. They simply understood principles too frequently lost today . . . honor flowed in the midst of their desperation, and both received a full reward.

Honor Principle

As you scan the Gospels you find others who received partial, full, or no reward. Each incident uniquely reflects their stewardship of honor. For some there is a glaring lack of due honor; for others there is cordial or abundant honor; and for still others there is blatant dishonor as they approached Jesus. If honor isn't immediately apparent in the passages, the pattern or principle yet remains; it's a spiritual law, for God says,

> "Those who honor Me I will honor, and those who despise Me shall be lightly esteemed."
>
> —1 Sam. 2:30

Honor is an essential key to receiving from heaven. I like to refer to the above verse as "the honor principle." Those who honor God will be honored. That's just the way it works. Everyone who honored Jesus received from God in the proportion the honor was rendered. Think of it . . . not only were a servant and a daughter healed, but we are still celebrating their choices and faith today!

This principle is particularly highlighted just before the Passion. Jesus was at the house of Simon the leper in Bethany. As He reclines at the table, a woman approaches Him with an alabaster box of costly spikenard oil. The price of this perfume was a year's wages for a normal workingman. After weeping to wash Jesus' feet, she dries them with her hair, then breaks open the spikenard and pours it on Jesus' head.

She honored Jesus by lavishly anointing Him, but not all rejoiced at this outpouring: "But there were some who were indignant among themselves, and said, 'Why was this fragrant oil wasted?' For it might have been sold for more than three hundred denarii and given to the poor.' And they criticized her sharply" (Mark 14:4–5).

Outside the moment their observations sound so rational and

even thoughtful. How Christian to be thinking of the poor . . . yet they missed the bigger picture, something transpired in that moment. There had been an opportunity to honor the God of heaven and earth by honoring His Son, Jesus. Listen to the Master's sharp rebuke:

> Let her alone; why are you troubling her? She has done a good and beautiful thing to Me [praiseworthy and noble]. For you always have the poor with you, and whenever you wish you can do good to them; but you will not always have Me. She has done what she could. . . . And surely I tell you, wherever the good news (the Gospel) is proclaimed in the entire world, what she has done will be told in memory of her.
>
> —Mark 14:6–9 (AMP)

Wow, did you hear how He praised her? Many did great things in the days of Jesus, but none was honored in this manner, or to this degree. Jesus prophesied that her good and beautiful act of honor would be lauded everywhere the gospel would reach, not only in their time period but from generation to generation forevermore!

Her desire was to honor the Master, but this outpouring of anointing positioned her to be honored by the Master. The *honor principle* will always apply, always remain valid. God says, "Those who honor me I will honor, but those who despise me will be *disdained*" (1 Sam. 2:30, NIV, emphasis mine). Notice those who do not honor Him will be lightly esteemed. However, the NIV uses the word *disdained*, which is defined as "the feeling that someone is unworthy of one's consideration or respect." God considers those who dishonor Him as beneath His notice. This would imply a disregard for their needs and prayers.

Hear what Jesus says: "He who receives Me receives Him who sent Me" (John 13:20). In the context of what Jesus is saying, to receive someone is to honor him. So Jesus is actually saying, "He who honors Me honors the Father who sent Me." This is why He clearly tells us, "He who does not honor the Son does not honor the Father who sent Him" (John 5:23).

Those who honored Jesus were actually honoring the Father without knowing it. Jesus said, "I do not receive honor from men" (John 5:41); in His heart and mind it all went to the Father. He was not yet glorified. Once He was glorified decrees were made by the Father to the Son such as, "Let all the angels of God worship Him" (Heb. 1:6), and "Your throne, O God, is forever and ever; a scepter of righteousness is the scepter of Your kingdom" (Heb. 1:8; see also Phil. 2:8–10). Once glorified, He is worshipped as the Father is worshipped.

Yet while Jesus walked the earth He lived and ministered as the *Son of Man*. Philippians 2:6–7 in the Amplified Bible states, "Who, although being essentially one with God and in the form of God . . . stripped Himself [of all privileges and rightful dignity], so as to assume the guise of a servant (slave), in that He became like men and was born a human being." So as a Man He continually passed all honor that was given Him along to the Father in His heart. This is why He continually addressed people He healed with statements such as, "See that you tell no one; but go your way, show yourself to the priest, and offer the gift that Moses commanded, as a testimony to them" (Matt. 8:4). And again we read, "Jesus sternly warned them, saying, 'See that no one knows it'" (Matt. 9:30); and similar references are found all over the Gospels.

While here Jesus was earth's connection to the Father; therefore a tangible way to honor the Father was by the treatment of His Son. This is why there was no rebuke for the unnamed woman who honored Jesus the Son with her costly ointment. He never rebuked those who honored Him; but rather praised them for making this connection with the Father. Understand He wasn't seeking His own honor, but rather modeling the *Honor Principle* to the ones He was sent to.

The Flow of Honor

The week Jesus was crucified He made this profound statement in regard to how His ministry would continue even after His departure:

> "I tell you, you will not see me again until you say, 'Blessed is he who comes in the name of the Lord.'"
>
> —Luke 13:35 (NIV)

In other words, "You will not see Me again until you recognize those I send you by declaring, 'Blessed is the one who comes in the name of the Lord.'" Or to put it yet another way, "You will not perceive or see Me again until you *honor* those I send in My name." Stop and meditate on this. Jesus said He would manifest Himself when we bless or honor the ones He sends. Why? Jesus answers this for us in other portions of the Scriptures. One such statement is, "Most assuredly, I say to you, he who receives (*honors*) whomever I send receives (*honors*) Me; and he who receives (*honors*) Me receives (*honors*) Him who sent Me" (John 13:20, words in parentheses mine).

In light of this, hear what Jesus further says in regard to applying the honor principle to everyday life:

> "He who receives you receives Me, and he who receives Me receives Him who sent Me. He who receives a prophet in the name of a prophet shall receive a prophet's reward. And he who receives a righteous man in the name of a righteous man shall receive a righteous man's reward. And whoever gives one of these little ones only a cup of cold water in the name of a disciple, assuredly, I say to you, he shall by no means lose his reward."
>
> —Matthew 10:40–42

Without changing the meaning, allow me to insert the word *honor* everywhere the words *receives* and *gives* occurs in these verses.

"He who *honors* you *honors* Me, and he who *honors* Me *honors* Him who sent Me. He who *honors* a prophet in the name of a prophet shall receive a prophet's reward. And he who *honors* a righteous man in the name of a righteous man shall receive a righteous man's reward. And whoever *honors* one of these little ones *with* only a cup of cold water in the name of a disciple, assuredly, I say to you, he shall by no means lose his reward."

To gain a proper frame of reference, there are two major points that require addressing in these verses. First, there is an authority structure in the kingdom of God. It begins with the Father and flows down to Jesus, the One He sent and gave all authority to. After His resurrection Jesus declared, "All authority has been given to Me in heaven and on earth" (Matt. 28:18). He is the head of the church, and the day will come when He presents the Kingdom back to His Father once all rebellion has been placed under His feet (see 1 Cor. 15:24–26).

Next in this order of kingdom authority is the "prophet." Bear in mind, Jesus was speaking to a people who didn't possess New Testament Scriptures. They were unfamiliar with our terminology and ways, so He spoke in terms familiar to them.

Prophets in the Old Testament functioned as the Lord's spokespersons (see Ex. 4:16; 7:1). Hebrews 1:1–2 further confirms this: "God, who at various times and in various ways spoke in time past to the fathers by the prophets, has in these last days spoken to us by His Son." And the New Testament reiterates this with how once Jesus was raised from the dead and ascended on high: "He Himself gave some to be apostles, some prophets, some evangelists, and some pastors and teachers" (Eph. 4:11).

If Jesus were addressing us today He might say it like this: "He who honors an apostle in the name of an apostle will receive an apostle's reward; he who honors a pastor in the name of a pastor will receive a pastor's reward"—the same being true of prophets, evangelists, or teachers.

In Matthew 10, Jesus moves on from honoring a prophet (or those in leadership), to a righteous man, and then finishes with honoring the "little ones." He in effect covered all bases and authority dynamics believers come in contact with—those above us in authority, those on our level, and finally those under our care or delegated authority. Every human being we encounter falls under one of these three areas.

This brings us to the second major point. If we honor those above us . . . we receive a reward. If we are honorable with those on our level (our peers) . . . we receive a reward. And finally, by honoring those under our care or authority . . . we receive a reward as well. Remember our paraphrase, "You will not see Me again until you *honor* the ones I send in My name." If we couple this with the verses in Matthew, we discover that each of these three levels carries an amazing reward from heaven. Also, these rewards will always carry greater revelations of insight into who Jesus is. This will be our focus for the remainder of the book.

CHAPTER 4

Little to Do with the Leader

⌘

In the first three chapters we've covered large amounts of scripture in order to establish the vital role of honor in receiving from God. To quickly recap, the apostle John instructed us to diligently live in such a way to receive a *full reward*. For him to specifically write "full reward" tells us there is also a partial and no-reward scenario. In the ministry of Jesus we've seen there were some who received full, some partial, and others, no rewards; and it all boiled down to how they received (honored) Him.

Jesus stated just before His departure, "I'm going away and you will not see Me again until you honor the One I send you in My name" (author's paraphrase of Luke 13:35). He further shows if we honor a leader we will receive the reward God has to give through the leader; again the same with those who are our peers; and finally the same with those under our authority. We'll address those in authority first, and then discuss the other two levels in later chapters.

Examples of Our Day

I'm personally acquainted with ministers who travel extensively in preaching the gospel. First who come to mind is a husband and wife team, T. L. and Daisy Osborn. Lisa and I had the privilege of serving them numerous times back in the mid-eighties. In those days I worked for a church of eight thousand members; my job was to host all the guest speakers. The Osborns came in for several occasions, so we were able to spend considerable time together. We became close and frequently wrote and talked on the phone. Twice T.L. sent me boxes of his clothes; we were the same size. He was, and still is, one of my heroes in the faith.

At that time, T.L. and Daisy had already led millions of souls to salvation. This was accomplished not through television, but rather in their open-air crusades around the world. Most, however, were conducted in the continent of Africa. Anywhere from 50,000 to 250,000 attended each of their meetings.

In each of their meetings several people with blind eyes were opened. People who had arrived with absolutely no vision left with the ability to see! But this is only the tip of the iceberg. Hundreds of deaf ears were opened; scores were healed of incurable diseases; numerous people who were crippled and carried to their crusades on stretchers left walking and carrying their beds home. Brother Osborn has written volumes sharing the notable miracles of healings that have occurred in their open-air meetings, especially in Africa.

One of the most moving stories I remember them sharing with us involved a lady visiting Daisy in between meetings at a crusade in Africa. She was carrying a dead baby. in her arms. The baby was completely wrapped up in a blanket, even the face. The mother gave the baby to Daisy and asked through the interpreter to please pray for her child that he might live. Daisy took the bundled-up corpse in her arms and began to utter a simple prayer. Within moments she felt movement and heard coughing and sneezing under the blanket. She opened the blanket, and there staring at her was the alive baby boy.

Daisy then covered the child back up and handed him back to his mother. The mother lifted the blanket, and upon seeing his face broke out with shouts of excitement.

This puzzled Daisy. She wondered why the mother didn't react when she heard the baby coughing and sneezing while in her arms. Why wasn't it until the mother lifted the blanket to see his face that she was overcome with joy?

So Daisy asked the mother through the interpreter. The response from the mother was, "My baby was born with only one eye. There was only an empty socket where the other eye was to be. When I looked just now, my child stared back at me with two beautiful eyes!"

There are so many other amazing stories of the mighty works done by them, all in the name of Jesus Christ our risen Savior.

I have another friend who does numerous crusades in Africa, particularly in Ethiopia and Sudan. His crusades range anywhere from 50,000 to 200,000 people. In his meetings he also sees hundreds of eyes and ears opened. He sees crippled people walk, numerous diseases cured, and tumors shrink and disappear.

A few years ago he told me a most profound story. In the area of Africa in which he was conducting his crusade, there was a man known as "Monkey Man." He was so demon possessed that no one could tame him. He lived naked in trees and walked on his hands and feet. His hands were as calloused as his feet.

Some caring locals harnessed and brought him to the meeting. My friend told me, "John, I was just preaching to a large crowd, and suddenly I saw a man just fly up in the air—it must have been eight feet—and just suddenly drop to the ground. He wasn't moving. I thought he was dead. The next day he was on my platform fully dressed in a suit testifying how God had delivered him; it was 'Monkey Man.'"

He then told me the crowd went from tens of thousands to hundreds of thousands because "Monkey Man" was known throughout the area. The masses wanted to hear the Word of God that liberated this prisoner of demonic powers.

I could give numerous stories of men and women who see these kinds of mighty works, especially in Africa. However, the point is these same ministers come back to America or other Western nations; same person, same message, same anointing, same ministry technique, yet there are only a few headaches, bad backs, or some cases of arthritis healed in their meetings. Why? It revolves around *honor!* These friends I speak of are treated in some of these nations with such high esteem. They are seen as men and women sent from God, and are treated as royalty.

"You're the Man of God, Aren't You?"

On a few occasions I've also ministered in Africa, countries like Kenya, Zimbabwe, Angola, and others. Often I'm almost uncomfortable with the way I'm hosted (not to their discredit, but to my comfort level). They treat me like they would a king. My hosts put me up in their finest hotels, and I know it is a very great stretch for them financially. They will not let me carry a thing, not even my Bible. They will give me their finest food, and their best people will serve me.

I recall one time after preaching to several thousand being taken back to an air-conditioned room (few in the meetings had ever experienced air-conditioning at all). A woman surrounded by others who were there to serve came up and knelt before me with her head bowed and held out a big basin while another woman held a pitcher of water to wash my hands. After washing my hands for me another took a towel from her arm and wiped my hands dry. They were giving me their finest; honoring me.

When that woman knelt before me I was uncomfortable. I thought, *I can wash my own hands; you don't need to do this.* Then it was as if the Holy Spirit sternly warned me, "Don't even think of refusing them. Let them serve you."

There is a difference between honor and worship. Forever and ever we will worship *only* our God, Lord and King. However, forever and ever we'll give honor to whom honor is due. It's proper protocol in the kingdom of God.

I recall in the 1990s having the privilege of speaking to a well-known apostle's leadership. This man has over five million people in the churches he oversees. His churches are in eighteen different nations on the continent of Africa. Every February he gathers all six thousand senior pastors together (no associate pastors are invited) and asks leaders from America and other continents to come in and speak to his pastors. It was one of the strongest anointings I recall operating under in the entire decade of the nineties. I preached literally like a man from another world. The presence of God was mind-blowing.

In between the meetings I was being served in a manner similar to what I've just described. After the person walked away this leader looked at me and said, "Do you see the person who just did that for you? He's the head of the CIA of the entire nation."

I was in shock. After regaining my composure, I uttered back in disbelief, "And he just did that for me?" I couldn't believe someone of that importance would perform such a simple service for me. I should be honored to sit in his presence, let alone have him serving me.

This great apostle then stared back at me with a puzzled look and said, "You're the man of God, aren't you?" I thought, *We Americans just don't get it.*

How a Messenger Is Received

I've been traveling and ministering the Word of God for over twenty years. I've consistently noticed the places where it is easiest to minister (the greatest impact and miracles; the easiest to preach; and the strongest presence of God) are in various developing nations, prisons, and military bases. Why? Because most often they show honor and revere authority.

I remember when I discovered it really had nothing to do with me as the minister, but rather the people's reception. I was scheduled to speak in a church in the southeastern part of the United States. Also located in this community was the state's highest-security prison, which contained roughly fifteen hundred men. The senior pastor of the church was also the assistant prison chaplin. He asked me if I would consider speaking to the prisoners Sunday morning. Their service started at 8:00 a.m. and the church service didn't start until 11:00; we had ample time to do both. I gladly agreed.

Over one hundred prisoners attended that Sunday-morning service. The worship was amazing; the men were singing with all their hearts. I lost sight of the fact it was a maximum-security prison until after the service when I asked the praise-and-worship leader how long he was in for. He had such clear eyes and a cheerful countenance; I thought I would hear him say two or three years.

He looked at me with great peace and humility and said, "Sir, I'm in for three life sentences." Needless to say I was in absolute shock. His treatment toward me was of the utmost respect. This also is what I sensed in every one of these men who were in attendance. These prisoners were amazed that an out-of-town minister would take the time to come and tell them about Jesus. The honor they gave me was remarkable. I was truly humbled by their reception.

Once I took the microphone that morning I immediately started teaching and preaching like a man from another world. The anointing was so strong, the energy so abundant, I was running around like a football coach readying his team for the championship game. The men were shouting enthusiastically; it was a bang-up time!

I spoke for an hour, then the Spirit of God fell in that auditorium, and for the next hour and a half amazing things happened. Men were saved, filled with the Holy Spirit, healed, and called into full-time ministry.

My traveling assistant came up at the end of the service, took the microphone, and with tears running down his cheek said with passion, "If I lived in this community, this would be my home church." An enormous shout erupted; the men went wild with joy.

We left the prison at 10:30. The pastor, my assistant, and I were so pumped. We were all commenting with anticipation how great the service would be at the pastor's church. I said, "This service is going to be so good after what we've been in." I just knew we would arrive and the glory on us would overflow right into that church's service.

I'll never forget what happened. I walked into that service and could barely speak. The atmosphere was so hard and oppressive I was hindered in my preaching. I kept thinking, *Wait a minute, less than two hours ago I was speaking and ministering like a man from another world. What is going on?* I couldn't figure it out. I couldn't work it up or stir it up within me. I was stifled. The anointing on my life was restrained. I didn't understand at that time the honor principle. I was in the process of learning. Now I want everyone to know!

Let's put a cap on the magnitude of what happened in this prison. Sixteen years later, I was asked to speak at a large church in Omaha, Nebraska. I wasn't aware of the treat awaiting me. In the first service I did for this church I discovered that the man running the soundboard, who was one of the church's full-time staff members, was the man who led praise and worship in the prison that Sunday morning. I was both shocked and elated. I asked, "How did you get out? You were in for three life sentences with no eligibility for parole."

He proceeded to tell me the miracle of his release, which is too in-depth to write at this time. However, he showed me a prophetic word I'd given him in the middle of our service sixteen years earlier. The prison service was recorded on tape, which gave him the ability to write down what was said. He kept it in a journal all those years. He handed me his journal, and I proceeded to read what I said to him in that prison years earlier. My words stated that God was going to put him into full-time Kingdom service, and his ministry within the four walls of the prison was only preparation for his later ministry on the outside. I said this to him before I knew he was in for three life sentences. I'm so glad I didn't know his situation during the service; it would have been hard to say those words knowing the severity of his sentence.

This shows how powerful the movement of God was in this prison service and yet less than an hour later, in the church, the atmosphere was hard and I was stifled. I could barely preach. I learned that day it had nothing to do with me but how I'm received as one sent by God. The prisoners valued, honored, esteemed me. The church members said with their body language, "We've heard it all. We've heard many guest ministers; what do you have to say that's any different?" The vast difference of results stemmed from one word—honor.

Honoring When Insulted

Allow me to further show from Scripture that it has very little to do with the minister, but rather how the leader is received. There was a man in the Old Testament whose name was Elkanah. He had two wives, Hannah and Peninnah. (I'm so glad we don't do that now. I love being married to one woman.)

Peninnah had children, but Hannah had none; she was barren. In those days women showed their love for their husbands by giving them children, especially males. Why? Because it was so important to carry on the man's posterity.

Year after year the family would travel to Shiloh to sacrifice to the Lord. The number of Peninnah's children continued to increase, while Hannah would have no one to present to the Lord. This embarrassed Hannah, and to make matters worse Peninnah taunted her. Scripture records, "And her rival also provoked her severely, to make her miserable" (1 Sam. 1:6). Can you imagine the driving insults of Peninnah: "Hey girl, who loves our husband? I've given him all these children. And you, where are your children? You're no woman; you're not even half a woman. Does our husband despise you in the bedroom? Are you unattractive to him? He sure loves me." On and on she went.

Finally, one year Hannah had enough. She decided to go to the tabernacle and find comfort in the presence of the Lord away from her adversary. She was in distress, and in the process of praying to the Lord, weeping bitterly.

Hannah spoke from her heart; her lips moved but no words were coming out. She was making a petition to the Lord; if He would open her womb and give her a child, she would give the child back to the Lord for the rest of his life, and forever.

Meanwhile Eli, the head priest, was sitting by and noticed her manner. He thought she was intoxicated with alcohol, and said to her, "Hey, woman, how long will you be drunk, get rid of your wine!" (see 1 Samuel 1:13–14).

Once again, I'm glad Hannah wasn't American. If so, Eli might have gotten an earful. She most likely would have been enraged, thinking, *What kind of priest is this? I'm pouring my heart out to God and fasting and he accuses me of being drunk. No, this can't be right, my ears are deceiving me. I'm only imagining I heard this, right? But no, he really did say it. How cruel, ungodly, insensitive. What a jerk. How can he be the head of this tabernacle? This guy needs to be told off, fired, thrown out of ministry!*

She then could have easily blurted out, "Did you just call me drunk? I'm fasting and pouring my heart out to God for a need in my life and you accuse me of being intoxicated. You can't even recognize when someone is earnestly seeking God? What kind of a priest are you, what kind of a tabernacle is this? I'm going to tell my husband and we are getting out of here. We're going to the tabernacle down the street!"

Had Hannah done this she would have never received her reward. She would have never had a child and could have easily grown bitter toward the Lord. She would have died one day, saying God doesn't answer prayer. *I fasted, I prayed diligently, but God didn't reply.* However, this isn't what Hannah did. Hear her reply to the leader who insulted her: "No, my lord, I am a woman of sorrowful spirit. I have drunk neither wine nor strong drink, but I was pouring out my soul before the Lord. Regard not your handmaid as a wicked woman" (1 Sam. 1:15–16, AMP).

You can see she honored him greatly. She first of all calls him "my lord." She then referred to herself as his "handmaid." She did nothing but speak to him with the utmost respect. She honored him. Eli then said to her: "Go in peace, and may the God of Israel grant your petition which you have asked of Him" (v. 17, AMP).

In the next three months Hannah became pregnant, and within one year gave birth to baby Samuel. He was the one who would bring revival to all Israel. What Hannah desired and prayed to receive for years wasn't manifested until she honored the priest who slighted her; of whom God later said, "I have warned him continually that judgment is coming for his family, because his sons are blaspheming God and he hasn't disciplined them. So I have vowed that the sins of Eli and his sons will never be forgiven" (3:13–14, NLT).

Wow, that is something you never want to hear God say about you or your family. No forgiveness forever! Yet Hannah receives from God by honoring this man. It had very little to do with what Eli did, but rather how Hannah received the man who was over her in authority. If we honor those who are over us, we receive the reward God gives through their position.

CHAPTER 5

Authority

∞

Before continuing to discuss a prophet or leader's reward, we must first cover the importance or value of authority. Once this truth is established in our hearts we can sincerely and more effectively honor those over us.

Recall the meaning of *honor*; it is "to value, see as weighty and precious." If the object of our honor is a person in authority, a subject we are addressing in the next few chapters, honor carries the meaning of respect and even reverence. *Webster's Dictionary* (1828 version) defines *honor* as "to revere, respect; *to treat with deference and submission*, and *perform relative duties to*." From this definition we further see submission to authority is an aspect of true honor.

To say we honor authority, yet refrain from submission and obedience to it, is to deceive ourselves. To honor authority is to submit to authority; we dishonor authority by not submitting to it. Recall the Roman officer; he was a man who recognized, acknowledged, and submitted to authority. It was a part of his being; it was in his heart. Consequently he greatly honored Jesus and received a full reward.

Four Divisions of Authority

It is easy to have little or no regard for Kingdom-delegated authority without a firm understanding of it, especially in our society today. Our hearts must be established in this truth. We are concisely told:

> "Let every soul be subject to the governing authorities. For there is no authority except from God, and the authorities that exist are appointed by God. Therefore whoever resists the authority resists the ordinance of God."
>
> —Rom. 13:1–2

First, notice this is not a suggestive comment. It's not advice; it is a command. Also notice the words "every soul." This means there are no exceptions. All who call upon the name of Jesus are to adhere to this charge.

Who are these "governing authorities"? In this specific text Paul is referring to civil or governmental authorities. However, these words of exhortation apply not only to governmental leaders but also other areas of delegated authority.

The New Testament speaks of four divisions of delegated authority: civil, church, family, and social. In speaking of social I include employers, bosses, teachers, coaches, and so on. The New Testament gives specific guidelines for each area, however; in most cases, the counsel spans the borders and extends to all areas of delegated authority.

Recall, in speaking of receiving a prophet in the name of a prophet, Jesus coupled this with a righteous man, and finally a little one. As stated earlier, from this we see the three levels of human beings we encounter: those above us, those on our level, and those entrusted to our authority. In regard to those above us, even though He speaks of a "prophet," which specifically addresses church authority, the principles span the borders and extend to all areas of authority. The following scriptures confirm this:

That is also why you pay taxes, because the authorities are working for God when they fulfill their duties. Pay, then, what you owe them; pay them your personal and property taxes, *and show respect and honor for them all.*

—Romans 13:6–7 (TEV, emphasis mine)

Civil authorities are appointed by God and are working for Him. In honoring them we honor Him who appointed them; God in turn will honor us. It's the honor principle. In regard to social authority we read:

Let as many as are servants under the yoke count their own masters worthy of all *honor.*

—1 Timothy 6:1 (ASV, emphasis mine)

This would practically read for us today, "Let as many as are employees under hire count their employers or bosses worthy of all honor." Or it could read, "Let as many as are students under education count their teachers worthy of all honor." It would be the same for athletes and coaches or other types of relationships involving one submitting to another. In regard to family authority we read:

"Honor your father and mother," which is the first commandment with promise: "that it may be well with you and you may live long on the earth."

—Ephesians 6:2–3 (emphasis mine)

The reward for honoring our parents is attached to the command. We will discuss this in more depth later. And finally, in regard to church authority we read:

Dear brothers and sisters, *honor* those who are your leaders in the Lord's work. They work hard among you and warn you against all that is wrong. Think highly of them and give them your wholehearted love.

—1 Thessalonians 5:12–13 (NLT, emphasis mine)

There are more scriptures pertaining to each area of authority, and we'll bring them up later. The point is, God tells us to honor each area of delegated authority and in doing so the honor principle applies. We will be rewarded; whether partial or full, however, is determined by the degree we value the authority.

A Kingdom

We must remember the kingdom of God is just that, a kingdom. It has rank, order, and delegated authority. I've said this for years, but in preaching the gospel all over the world, on every continent (except Antarctica), I've found the most difficult people in the world to communicate the things of God to are those of the Western world. Why? The answer is elementary.

We are a people trying to understand Kingdom principles with a democratic mind-set.

The kingdom of God is not a democracy. So if we relate to God with a democratic mind-set we will not connect with Him. We will be without the protection of His authority and can be easily misled. Could this be why Jesus said so many in our generation would be deceived? Today, more than ever, we disregard authority in our culture; but what's more alarming, it's not just our society, but among professing believers as well. We must always keep in mind all legitimate authority is from God, and is given for protection, provision, and peace.

This Western mind-set is the cause for most church splits in

America, and why so many people are resorting to home churches. These professing believers do not want to be under the authority established by Jesus Christ Himself. You may say, *But John, the Chinese church exists in home churches.* Yes, that is true, but they were forced to because they could not meet in public. They are also extremely organized according to the principles of the Word of God. There's an amazing authority structure. Just this year I've been asked to meet with five leaders of the underground church in China. These five men are responsible for overseeing tens of millions of lives. They are the leading elders of the underground church. They are so organized, our ministry sent two hundred and fifty thousand books into their churches and every book was distributed within a few days. They have structure that flows in line with biblical authority.

Most home churches popping up in America are not this way. They lack true New Testament government and accountability. If you notice in the Epistles, Paul continually told men like the apostles Titus and Timothy to set up elders in the churches they were sent to, and these leaders were to correct, rebuke, exhort, and build up the churches. There was an answerability set up by the authority structure Jesus established. You don't readily find this in home churches in this nation. Rather you find many believers who have been hurt or offended and are therefore disillusioned with church structure. They've resorted to home churches in order to live without accountability.

We must remember Jesus is the One who established the church, not man. If you read the book of Acts you'll notice the believers met corporately and in every house. It is good to meet in homes, but our leadership and accountability must come from the local church body, which is headed up by appointed elders.

All Legitimate Authority Is from God

Returning to the scripture in Romans, every one of us is to be subject to governing authorities. Why? It's because "there is no authority except from God" (13:1). All legitimate authority in the universe has its origin from the throne of God. If you are truly born of the Spirit of God, you will recognize and esteem authority. In fact, show me a person who has no regard for authority and I will show you a person who is not a child of God. It doesn't matter if he has prayed the sinner's prayer and goes to church weekly. He who has no honor in his heart for authority is not saved.

You may ask, "John, how can you be so bold to say that?" Jesus said we would know true believers by their fruits, not by the fact they've prayed a formulaic prayer. A person who truly knows and loves God is a person who recognizes His authority, because to know God is to know authority. God and His authority are inseparable.

Paul further states in Romans, "The authorities that exist are appointed by God" (13:1). Do you notice it doesn't say authorities are elected or selected by people? No, God Himself appoints them. In fact, the English word *appointed* in this verse is the Greek word *tasso*, which means "to assign, ordain, or set." In no way does this word have "by chance" implications. It is direct appointment. Since God has appointed all authorities, we refuse the Authority behind them if we dishonor or refuse to submit to them. Whether we know it or not, we resist the ordinance or rule of God. When we oppose God's delegated authority, we oppose God Himself. This is why the apostle writes, "Whoever resists the authority resists the ordinance of God" (13:2).

I recall when I first became aware of this truth. In 1992 Bill Clinton was elected president of the United States. I was depressed and angry for about three days. Then the Holy Spirit got it across to me that no one gets into office without Him knowing it. As a result of this revelation in my heart, I went from being critical of President Clinton to revering, praying, and thanking God for him. God tells us through the apostle Paul, "I exhort first of all that supplications, prayers, intercessions, and giving of thanks be made for . . . all who are in authority, that we may lead a quiet and peaceable life in all godliness and reverence" (1 Tim. 2:1–2).

Notice a peaceable life is lived in reverence for authority. That's one of the rewards God gives those who honor authority. If we as believers do not honor those in authority, we'll bring problems on ourselves.

There are two types of persecution. One is self-inflicted; the other is for righteousness' sake. The apostle Peter addresses both; in regard to the first he states, "There's no particular virtue in accepting punishment that you well deserve" (1 Pet. 2:20, The Message). Simply put, if we do what is wrong, we will be punished for it. Or to make it even plainer, if you see red and blue flashing lights in your rearview mirror after running a stop sign, don't blame the devil. Why? This is one reason God has set up authorities, "For the authorities do not frighten people who are doing right, but they frighten those who do wrong. So do what they say, and you will get along well" (Rom. 13:3, NLT). So it's quite easy to eliminate self-inflicted persecution; just obey authority and you'll have no problems.

The other type of persecution is for righteousness' sake. This is when we are punished by authorities even when what we did was right. Peter says it this way: "But if you're treated badly for good behavior and continue in spite of it to be a good servant, that is what counts with God. This is the kind of life you've been invited into, the kind of life Christ lived" (1 Pet. 2:20–21, The Message).

When we are mistreated and continue to be a good worker, student, civilian, church member, etc., this is honor at its highest. It takes the fear of the Lord in our hearts to continue to treat as valuable those who have mistreated us.

Instead of adhering to these words, many today protest, "I'm free, I'm a Christian, I live in a free country, I don't have to put up with this nonsense!" Yes, you are free, but remember what God's Word also states: "For you, brethren, have been called to liberty; only do not use liberty as an opportunity for the flesh" (Gal. 5:13). We are called to live a life of handling unfair treatment correctly. Listen to what Peter goes on to say, "For even to this were you called [it is inseparable from your vocation]. For Christ also suffered for you, leaving you [His personal] example, so that you should follow in His footsteps" (1 Pet. 2:21, AMP).

What was Jesus' example? He was punished by authorities for doing wrong when all He did was right. This sets up the age-old question. Should we submit to and even honor ungodly authorities, especially when they mistreat us?

Ungodly Authority?

Many have said to me in protest, "But John, I know some very harsh and even wicked authorities. Are you telling me God appoints them? And further, are we to submit to them? Aren't there exceptions to this?"

It is true. There are many authorities who are mean, tyrannical, and unjust; in fact the Scriptures are full of them. We must bear in mind what God's Word states. It tells us *all authority is of God*, but it does not say *all authority is godly*.

God knew when He had the writers of the New Testament instruct His children to submit to authority there would be ungodly authorities. In fact, there had already been many ungodly authorities recorded in Scripture. Look at Pharaoh. He cruelly treated the descendants of Abraham, God's covenant people. He suppressed them, beat them, and even killed their children.

Where did Pharaoh get his authority? According to Scripture, God told Pharaoh, "I have raised you up" (Ex. 9:16). Paul confirmed this in one of his epistles (see Rom. 9:17), and a truth is established by the testimony of two witnesses (John 8:17). There is no doubt that God, not men or the devil, raised up and set Pharaoh in his position of authority. This correlates with the statement, "The authorities that exist are appointed by God" (Rom. 13:1).

Look at Nebuchadnezzar, king of Babylon. He destroyed Judah, plundering the temple and most all the homes of God's people. He eventually had an empire spanning the known world. He was so disobedient to God's ways, that during a time period of his rule, he became a mad man and was driven from mankind. He dwelled with the beasts of the field and ate grass like an ox; his body was wet with the dew of the morning till his hair had grown like eagles' feathers and his nails like birds' claws (see Dan. 4:33). Yet God clearly said of this man, "Behold, I will send and bring Nebuchadnezzar the king of Babylon, *My servant*, and will set his throne" (Jer. 43:10, emphasis mine). God called him "My servant" because again, "the authorities that exist are appointed by God."

Look at King Saul. I've heard many ministers state, "Saul was the people's choice, but David was God's choice." This is a very wrong assumption, not lining up with the counsel of God's Word. Statements of ignorance like this can hurt God's people, because it subtly communicates that some legitimate authorities can be appointed by man and not by God. This in turn leads people to withhold honor, to not submit to some authority, and in turn bring harm to themselves. Hear what God Himself said of this insecure, mad, and ungodly leader: "I greatly regret that I have set up Saul as king, for he has turned back from following Me" (1 Sam. 15:11).

Notice God said, "I have set up Saul as king." Not the people, but God appointed him. Again, this correlates with the statement, "the authorities that exist are appointed by God."

David, who is the only person in the Bible called "a man after God's heart," was placed under Saul's authority. And this was done after God said he greatly regretted setting up Saul as king. This was no accident, rather God's plan.

Saul treated him with kindness and favor in the beginning as long as David was serving his purpose. Once David was perceived to be a threat to Saul's security, Saul became violent with jealousy and sought to destroy David, so he had to flee into obscurity for his life.

For the next fourteen years David would live in caves, wildernesses, other remote places, and even a foreign land. Think of it. From the ages of sixteen to thirty David could not go to his home, not even for a visit. He was exiled from his own family members and all his childhood friends. He could no longer spend time with his best friend Jonathan, because it would make David vulnerable to Saul's attack on his life. Everything he cherished as a young man: all the securities, comforts, places of pleasure and enjoyment of his childhood were stripped away for a period of fourteen years, just because of the leader God placed him under. How could God do this to the man after His own heart?

Even after the Lord stated He regretted setting up Saul, David still honored and submitted himself to his king. David proved his innocence to Saul repeatedly, yet Saul continually sought his life. After a few years of exile David had an opportunity to end the misery created by his leader. In the wilderness of En Gedi an opportunity arose to kill Saul. The king and his army disarmed in the cave of En Gedi and were unaware David and his men were fully armed hiding in the back part of the cave. David's men encouraged him to kill Saul; they even misused God's word to urge him to do so, saying: "This is the day of which the LORD said to you, 'Behold I will deliver your enemy into your hand, that you may do to him as it seems good to you'" (1 Sam. 24:4).

They were in essence pleading, "David, King Saul is a maniac, he's destroying our nation, he has murdered innocent families and priests. The great prophet Samuel has anointed you to be the next leader of Israel, God has spoken it. If you don't kill him first, he will kill you. This is self-defense, any court of law would approve it and find you innocent!" This was excellent reasoning and they didn't have to mention the obvious: that Saul's unwarranted accusations and attacks against David made life miserable for him, and them.

Their pressure didn't persuade David, but it did give him an idea. He would prove once and for all his innocence to Saul by cutting off a corner of his robe. If Saul had proof David could kill him but restrained himself and his men, Saul would no longer be concerned that David would steal away his position of authority, and stop pursuing him to destroy his life.

Once he cut his leader's robe, Scripture says his heart was troubled, and his conscience stricken. He dishonored his king. How could he have done such a thing? He rebounded quickly by sternly commanding his men, "Stop talking foolishly. We're not going to attack Saul. He's my king, and I pray that the LORD will keep me from doing anything to harm His chosen king" (vv. 6–7, CEV).

However, since David had already done damage to the king's robe he decided to go ahead and show his innocence. He shouted from a distance to his leader,

"Why do you listen to the words of men who say, 'Indeed David seeks your harm'? Look, this day your eyes have seen that the LORD delivered you today into my hand in the cave, and someone urged me to kill you. But my eye spared you, and I said, 'I will not stretch out my hand against my lord, for he is the LORD's anointed.' Moreover, my father, see! Yes, see the corner of your robe in my hand! For in that I cut off the corner of your robe, and did not kill you, know and see that there is neither evil nor rebellion in my hand, and I have not sinned against you. Yet you hunt my life to take it. Let the LORD judge between you and me, and let the LORD avenge me on you. But my hand shall not be against you."

—1 Samuel 24:9–12

If there was any needed vengeance, which there certainly was, David trusted God for it. But as for his behavior, he did nothing but honor Saul. He even called the man who made his life miserable "my father."

Saul, greatly amazed at the goodness of David, cried back to him, "You are more righteous than I; for you have rewarded me with good, whereas I have rewarded you with evil" (v. 17). Saul then departed with his men.

David's Greatest Test of Honor

Now that David proved his innocence you would think Saul would leave him alone. Not a chance with this cruel leader. A short while later Saul heard David was hiding in the hills of Hachilah. So again, Saul took three thousand of Israel's finest warriors to hunt and destroy David.

Can you imagine the devastation of David's heart? He proved his innocence to Saul just a short while back, and now Saul continued to seek his life. This was sure evidence of what David hoped wasn't true: his leader was a cold-blooded murderer. This would enrage most. *I honored my leader by sparing his life when I could have easily taken it in self-defense; and this is what I get in return for the honor I've shown?* Many would sneer, "Now you'll really pay for this!"

Soon David learned Saul's army was put in a deep sleep from the Lord (see 1 Sam. 26:12). He asked his men who would be willing to sneak over to the camp of Saul. The perfect volunteer came forward, Abishai, Joab's little brother (they were bloodthirsty brothers).

So David and Abishai came to the campsite of Saul's army by night. Saul lay sound asleep in the middle of the camp next to Abner. Then Abishai said to David, "God has delivered your enemy into your hand this day. Now therefore, please, let me strike him at once with the spear" (v. 8).

I can just see David hesitating in his response. He's thinking, *I can end at this moment all my misery, not only mine, but my men's, and our beloved nation's. Here is one of my followers, who's been nothing but loyal to me, he's requesting of me to do the logical thing, not only for me, but all those who follow me. These faithful men would like to see their families again. Why should I be loyal to Saul and not to my men? Saul's lied to me. He's stolen my reputation by telling the nation I'm a traitor. He's stolen my privileges of a son in my father's house, and as a citizen of Israel. He's stolen my wife and given her to another man [see 1 Sam. 25:44]. He's taken all my possessions.*

His thoughts are interrupted by the voice of the one who's been so loyal to him, who's committed his life to David's well-being, Abishai. "David, what are you doing? Why are you hesitating to give me the command to execute this monster?"

I can see Abishai continuing. "Don't even tell me you're thinking of not doing this. You've proven your innocence time and time again. Remember back at the cave of En Getti; he was yours, yet you spared his life. You proved without a question your loyalty to him, and yet he continues to hunt your life. This is self-defense, it would stand up in any court of law."

Still no response.

Now I can see Abishai getting impatient. "David, you were anointed by the great prophet Samuel to be the next king of Israel. You are the one who is to deliver our people from this wicked king. Do you not recall he has murdered, in cold blood, eighty-five priests of Nob, their wives, and little babies, just because they gave us some bread to eat [see 1 Sam. 22]? He's a filthy murderer!"

Finally Abishai blurts out, "David, why do you think God put this entire army into a deep sleep? He did it so you could deliver our nation from this wicked king!"

David weighed out the counsel of his loyal friend. As logical as it sounded, it didn't line up with the counsel of God. So David cast off the words of Abishai, as well as his own thoughts of self-defense, and sternly charged, " 'You must not harm him! The LORD will certainly punish whoever harms his chosen king. By the living LORD,' David continued, 'I know that the LORD himself will kill Saul, either when his time comes to die a natural death or when he dies in battle. The LORD forbid that I should try to harm the one whom the LORD has made king!' " (1 Sam. 26:9–11, TEV).

David restrained his servant and both left the camp.

Why did God put the army into a deep sleep? To test David's heart. To see if he would remain a man after God's heart or become like Saul and take matters into his own hands. Would he dishonor God by dishonoring the one appointed by God? It was a life-defining moment for David.

David honored the king, even when the king did all he could to dishonor David. The reward would be greater than David imagined. For see what God said of this man who valued and respected his cruel leader:

> "I have found My servant David; with My holy oil I have anointed him, with whom My hand shall be established; also My arm shall strengthen him. The enemy shall not outwit him, nor the son of wickedness afflict him. I will beat down his foes before his face, and plague those who hate him. But My faithfulness and My mercy shall be with him. . . . Once I have sworn by My holiness; I will not lie to David; His seed shall endure forever, and his throne as the sun before Me; it shall be established forever like the moon, even like the faithful witness in the sky."
>
> —Psalm 89:20–24, 35–37

David saw beyond the cruelness of Saul, and saw the authority upon him. He lived in the honor principle; if he honored the one God set over him, he would be, in fact, honoring God Himself. And if he honored God then God would honor him. I would say the previous scripture shows the immense honor God showed David. Indeed, a great reward!

Shortly after this incident God did judge Saul; the Philistines killed him in battle. Once David heard the news of his death he wrote a love song to Saul and Jonathan, and then taught all the citizens of Judah to sing it. He honored his leader even after his leader was judged.

We've examined just a few biblical examples clearly showing it's God, not man or even demonic forces, who brings a human being into legitimate authority. Throughout the history of mankind, God has appointed every leader, whether their behavior has been good or harsh. He or she has been ordained for a specific reason, never by accident. Let me repeat again the infallible Word of God: "The authorities that exist are appointed by God."

In the case of a harsh leader, his or her authority is God appointed, however the cruel behavior is not originated by God. The leader will give an account to God, but in the meantime those who are under their rule will be tested, as was David. If they honor, they'll be greatly rewarded.

We've now seen that it is God who appoints all in authority. In the next chapter we'll continue to probe the question, are we to submit to authority, even if it is harsh or even wicked?

CHAPTER 6

Harsh Authority

∞

In the last chapter we learned from Scripture that God appoints all legitimate authorities, even the harsh ones. How can a good God appoint cruel people to positions of authority? The answer is simple: God is the originator of the authority, but He is not the author of the cruelty. Man is responsible for his cruel actions, not God. All authority is of God, but not all authority is godly.

Now we must address the other age-old question. Are we to submit to cruel authority when those in authority mistreat us? We can see the answer from David's life. His example displays that it is the will of God for us to submit to authority, even if it is ungodly. But let's take it one step further; let's hear it straight up. To do this we turn to the apostle Peter:

> "Servants (*employees, students, civilians, church members, etc.*), be submissive to your masters (*employers, bosses, teachers, church leaders, civil authorities*) with all fear, not only to the good and gentle, but also to the harsh."
>
> —1 Pet. 2:18 (words in parentheses mine)

Good and gentle leaders are great to have, and they are important for our development and growth. However, Peter not only points out the *good and gentle*, but also specifically states that we are to be submitted to the *harsh*.

Notice he says, "with all fear." In this lies the secret to what he commands. Recall that true honor originates from the heart and is an outflow of the fear of the Lord. We Americans tend to say to authorities, "You will have to earn my respect before I can honor and submit to you." However, according to the prophet Isaiah, the fear of the Lord does not judge by the seeing of the eye or the hearing of the ear; it judges according to righteous judgment (see Isa. 11:3). Therefore the fear of the Lord in a person's heart says to its leader, "I'm aware of the authority on you, that it originates from God. Therefore you already have my respect and honor. You don't have to earn it."

Notice again the end of his command: "not only to the good and gentle, but also to the *harsh*." One day while pondering this verse I thought, *Wait a minute, harsh? Maybe the New King James Version just got a little extreme with this word. Let me go to the Greek.*

The first dictionary I turned to was *Thayer's*; I discovered the Greek word for "harsh" is *skolios*. He defines this word as "crooked, perverse, wicked, unfair, and forward." I about jumped, thinking, *This is worse!* I thought, *Okay, maybe he missed it; I'll go to another*, hoping to find relief. I then turned to W. E. Vines, another expert in Greek New Testament words. He defines this word as "tyrannical or unjust masters (leaders)."

I continued to search. I found other translations were even harder than the NKJV. The New Century Version reads, "Not only those who are good and kind, but also those who are dishonest." The Contemporary English Version declares, "Do this, not only to those who are kind and thoughtful, but also to those who are cruel." The New American Standard Bible states "unreasonable."

Now we must ask, "Is God a child abuser?" No, a thousand times no! He is the best Dad in the universe. He doesn't just have love; He is Love. So let's process this: my loving heavenly Father is telling me, His child, to be submissive to a harsh, cruel, crooked, perverse, tyrannical, unjust, and dishonest leader? Why does He not only ask this of me, but command this of me? There are many reasons, but to sum them all up it can be said in one statement: *for my benefit.*

There are three benefits for honoring these leaders. First, if treated unfairly, our obedience to submit puts our case in the hands of God who will judge justly (see 1 Pet. 2:21–23). If we take matters in our own hands, God steps back and we are on our own, a miserable place to be. Most often, since it deals with authority, we will come out on the short end of the deal. On rare occasions we may win the battle, but a wound or root is left in our spirit that is not Christlike, that eventually brings trouble or even defilement, which manifests later.

Secondly, Peter tells us when we return honor or blessing for unfair treatment the following happens: "Do not repay evil with evil or insult with insult, but with blessing (*honor*), because to this you were called so that you may inherit a blessing" (1 Pet. 3:9, NIV, words in parentheses mine).

We are called to handle unfair treatment correctly by honoring (valuing, submitting, and blessing) those who are unkind to us. Why are we called to this? To position ourselves to receive a blessing (reward). So when you are mistreated, especially by someone in authority, you can get very excited because you are being set up for a reward!

A Reward of Promotion

I want to share a story I've written in a previous mini-book. This is a classic example showing how God sets up to reward us when we honor those who mistreat us.

I have a close friend, Al Brice, who is a pastor. Some years ago he pastored a church in Dallas and preached on a certain Sunday morning from the book of 1 Peter. When Al finished speaking, one of the members of the church (I'll call him Brian) approached him with an urgent question. "Pastor Brice," he said, "I am a junior executive for a very large insurance company. I have worked hard for years and was next in line to become vice president. All my fellow employees knew I had earned the promotion. I really deserved that job. But when the position came open, the company gave it to another man."

"Why did that happen?" Pastor Al asked.

"Because the other man is white and I'm black. Pastor, that's discrimination. And I believe I can prove it. In fact, I was getting ready to start legal action this coming week. But now you preached this message this morning and messed me up!"

Pastor Brice looked at Brian and said, "Do you want to do it God's way or do you want to do it your way?"

Without hesitation Brian answered, "Pastor, I love God with all my heart. I want to do it His way; that's why I'm here talking to you. Would you please pray with me?"

Al answered, "Yes," and they bowed their heads and committed his case into the hands of God the Father who would judge righteously.

The next morning Brian went to work and purposed to be the first to honor this fellow who had received the promotion. He went to the man's office, stuck out his hand, and said with a big smile, "I want to congratulate you on your promotion, and I just want you to know I'm going to be your best worker." You can imagine how uncomfortable this made the other guy, because he knew, too, the promotion went to the wrong person. Without events going the way they did, Brian would have been *his* boss and sitting behind that very desk.

Several weeks went by and nothing happened. You need to understand—that's often the case. God's judgment or deliverance will come, but it's often later than we would prefer! But Brian did not dwell on how he had been wronged. Rather he chose the route of honor. He continued performing his duties at a high level.

One day Brian got a call from a competitor, an extremely large international insurance company that had a branch office in Dallas. The man on the other end of the line said, "We've watched how you deal with mutual clients. We're very impressed. Would you be interested in coming to work for us?"

Brian didn't need to think long about this. "No, I'm not interested," he said. "I don't want to change jobs. I've been with this company for years. I have great benefits and a solid group of clients. My customers and fellow workers know my reputation and character. I'm in good shape. I really don't like change. Thank you, but I'm just not interested."

The man from the other company persisted. "Please, just meet us for one lunch so we can talk to you. What could be the harm in that?"

Brian tried to be even more firm. "I'm telling you, you're wasting your time. I'm not interested."

It was almost like the other guy was hard of hearing. "Oh, come on! Would you just give us one lunch?"

Almost in frustration, Brian said, "All right, I'll meet with you."

A time was set and the day of the lunch arrived. Brian and the others exchanged greetings and ordered their meals. One of the executives from the large insurance company said, "Brian, we have watched you and been so impressed with the way you handle your accounts. Our people have said, 'We would love for him to work for us.'"

Brian shook his head. "I told you before on the phone. You are wasting your time. I do not want to change jobs. I like stability. I have super benefits. I have so much invested with my company. I just don't want to do this."

"Okay, Brian, we hear you. But this is what we want you to do. Go home and talk to your wife. The two of you come up with a salary figure that you would like us to pay you. And then let's meet back here in a week and talk about it."

Almost against his better judgment, Brian sighed and said, "Well, all right."

He went home. He really had not taken any of this very seriously. He didn't even say much to his wife about the offer until the night before the next lunch. Brian was relaxing with his wife and finally said, "I really don't want to change jobs. They wanted us to name a salary number. I'm really tired of this, so this is what I'm going to do. I'll take them up on setting a salary and just do something ridiculous. I'll tell them I want a salary that is three times what I'm making now! They'll laugh me out of the restaurant and that will end this discussion real quick."

He wrote a short letter and put in the salary number that was triple his current pay. Keep in mind he was already quite high up in his company. Naming such a high number seemed ludicrous.

The next day Brian went to lunch. After the food was ordered, the insurance company executive asked Brian if he had come up with a salary request.

"I did," Brian said. He started reaching in his coat pocket to pull out the letter, but the other man stopped him. "No, no. We really don't want to see what you want us to pay you. We first want to show you what we want to pay you!"

The man slid a letter across the lunch table. Brian picked it up, and after reading a few lines, almost passed out. The number they were proposing was *four times* the salary he was making! Brian was so stunned he didn't know what to say. He just sat there staring at the letter. However, the men from the other insurance company misunderstood his speechlessness and concluded that maybe their offer wasn't high enough. So they upped their salary offer and added more benefits!

Finally, Brian regained his composure and said, "Gentlemen, I'm a Christian, so I want to take this offer home so I can pray about it with my wife. I'll get back with you."

"Sure, sure, take your time," the others said.

Brian went home and told his wife. They both prayed, and the Spirit of God spoke to both of them and the message from the Lord was, "Son, you put your case in My hands. I have vindicated you. This is My promotion. Take it!"

Now, years later, Brian doesn't live in Dallas anymore. He is a top executive of that giant insurance company at the international headquarters in Virginia. This company dwarfs the company Brian was working for when he was mistreated and did not get the promotion he deserved.

Now, what are we to conclude from this? Sure, Brian could have defended and even avenged himself. He had a legitimate legal case. He had rights he could have insisted on. He was dishonored and mistreated, and he possibly could have won the case. And even if he won the case he would not have been where he is today. He would have missed the blessing he was set up for! He chose to honor those in authority, even when mistreated, and not taking revenge and committing his case into the hands of God set him up for a full reward!

Submission versus Obedience

The third reason we are commanded to submit to harsh authorities is because in trusting God, rather than vindicating ourselves, godly character is built within us. Peter continues: "Therefore, since Christ suffered for us in the flesh, arm yourselves also with the same mind, for he who has suffered in the flesh has ceased from sin" (1 Pet. 4:1).

In the context of this epistle the suffering of Christ is mistreatment by authority. We are to arm ourselves with the same mind. Why? We are called to honor authority even when it mistreats us.

Peter states that if we do this we will cease from sin. Another way of saying this is that we will come to a place of spiritual maturity. Paul confirms this by writing, "We can rejoice, too, when we run into problems and trials, for we know that they are good for us—

they help us learn to endure. And endurance develops strength of character in us" (Rom. 5:3–4, NLT). As strength of character is built in us, it makes it easier to honor those who don't act in a manner that would merit honor. We are now walking in a greater measure of the fear of the Lord, which in turn will bring us greater rewards.

Now let's bring a proper scriptural balance to what we've been discussing. The Bible instructs us to unconditionally submit to authority; however, it does not teach us to unconditionally obey authority.

There is a difference between submission and obedience. Submission deals with our attitude, whereas obedience relates to our actions. This is why we are told, "If you are willing and obedient, you shall eat the good of the land" (Isa. 1:19). I recall once being corrected by the Holy Spirit. I was discouraged due to the fact things were not going well. For six months, I hadn't been receiving from God in my church; my pastor's messages hadn't been feeding me. In prayer the Lord pointed me to this scripture and told me this was the reason I wasn't receiving.

I countered, "I am obedient! I do everything my pastor and those over me tell me to do!"

The Holy Spirit quickly responded, "I didn't say, 'If you are obedient, you will eat the good of the land'; rather I said, 'If you are willing and obedient, you will eat the good of the land.' Obedience deals with your actions; willingness deals with your attitude. And your attitude stinks!"

I suddenly realized how important my heart attitude was. Again, remember this is where the fear of the Lord resides, and honor is an outflow of holy fear.

Again we see this in the New Testament. Paul states, "*Obey* those who rule over you, and be *submissive*, for they watch out for your souls, as those who must give account. Let them do so with joy and not with grief, for that would be unprofitable for you" (Heb. 13:17, emphasis mine). Notice he specifically states that we are to both obey and be submissive to those in authority over us. Obedience deals with our actions; submission deals with our attitude toward authority. Again, notice that if we don't honor those over us, it is unprofitable for us, not for the leader. We lose our reward.

As stated earlier, the Bible teaches unconditional submission to authority but not unconditional obedience. There is only one time—I repeat, one time—the Bible tells us not to obey an authority; and that is when authority tells us to sin (do something contrary to the written Word of God).

There are many scriptural examples of this; we'll look at just one. The king of Babylon, Nebuchadnezzar, made a decree that all the people were to bow and worship a golden image when they heard the sound of the musical instruments. The decree held consequences for those who refused; they would be tossed into a furnace.

At that time three Jewish young men were in his kingdom whose names were Shadrach, Meshach, and Abed-Nego. The king favored these men, as they were gifted and wise. However, these three men feared God, and their leader's decree directly violated the second commandment God gave Moses recorded in the Torah.

The three young men purposefully did not obey the king's decree. It was only a matter of time before their disobedience came to the attention of King Nebuchadnezzar. He was outraged by their actions and had them brought before him for questioning. Listen to their reply: "O Nebuchadnezzar, we do not need to defend ourselves before you. If we are thrown into the blazing furnace, the God whom we serve is able to save us. He will rescue us from your power, Your Majesty. But even if he doesn't, Your Majesty can be sure that we will never serve your gods or worship the gold statue you have set up" (Dan. 3:16–18, NLT).

They stood firm in obedience to God's command, yet spoke to the king with honor. They addressed him as "Your Majesty"; they didn't say, "You tyrant dog of a king, we'll never do what you say!" To speak in this manner of disrespect would have been dishonoring to God, who appointed this man to leadership. We are to submit to (honor) authority, even when we must disobey their command.

Shadrach, Meshach, and Abed-Nego honored God and the king. First, they honored God by refusing to sin, even when they knew they would face a horrible furnace. Second, they honored the king by submitting to his position of authority and speaking to him in a respectful way even when he spoke hatefully to them. They didn't in turn mock, ridicule, or threaten him in any way. They lived by the honor principle. Their reward would be both great and full, although it certainly didn't initially appear that way.

The king immediately commanded them to be hurled into the furnace. In fact he was so angry with them, he commanded the furnace to be heated up seven times its normal temperature. He then had mighty men of valor who were in his military take the three Jewish young men, bind them up in their clothes, and cast them into the furnace. The furnace was so hot it killed the military men who brought them to its entrance. We then read,

> And these three men, Shadrach, Meshach, and Abed-Nego, fell down bound into the midst of the burning fiery furnace.
>
> Then King Nebuchadnezzar was astonished; and he rose in haste *and* spoke, saying to his counselors, "Did we not cast three men bound into the midst of the fire?"
>
> They answered and said to the king, "True, O king."
>
> "Look!" he answered, "I see four men loose, walking in the midst of the fire; and they are not hurt, and the form of the fourth is like the Son of God."
>
> Then Nebuchadnezzar went near the mouth of the burning fiery furnace *and* spoke, saying, "Shadrach, Meshach, and Abed-Nego, servants of the Most High God, come out, and come *here*."
>
> Then Shadrach, Meshach, and Abed-Nego came from

the midst of the fire. And the satraps, administrators, gover-
nors, and the king's counselors gathered together, and they
saw these men on whose bodies the fire had no power; the
hair of their head was not singed nor were their garments
affected, and the smell of fire was not on them.

—Daniel 3:23–27

These three men not only escaped the horrible agony of the fire,
but they walked with a great angel from heaven in the furnace. They
were thrown in bound, but walked free in the furnace. Their ropes
were burned off, but their clothes were untouched. Once they came
out there wasn't even the smell of fire on them. Their reward manifested after they came out. We read,

> "Then the king promoted Shadrach, Meshach, and Abed-
> Nego in the province of Babylon."

—v. 30

They were promoted! When someone in authority mistreats us, if
we honor them we will be rewarded, just as the insurance executive
or the three Jewish young men we've just read about. It is a spiritual
law: by honoring those God appoints over us, we honor God; in
turn, God will honor us. Once we see beyond the circumstances and
focus on this spiritual law, we will never be disappointed.

For this reason Peter further writes, "And who is he who will
harm you if you become followers of what is good?" (1 Pet. 3:13).
In other words, once you get the honor principle deep within your
heart, what can anyone do to you? Any mistreatment, especially by
those in authority over you, is just setting you up for a promotion
or a reward if you handle the mistreatment correctly. So this is what
we must ask: how many rewards or promotions have we forgone
because we didn't walk in the honor principle?

CHAPTER 7

Honoring Civil Leaders

*For rulers are not to be feared by those who do good, but
by those who do evil. Would you like to be unafraid of
those in authority? Then do what is good, and they will
praise you, because they are God's servants working for
your own good. But if you do evil, then be afraid of them,
because their power to punish is real. They are God's
servants and carry out God's punishment on those who
do evil. For this reason you must obey the authorities—
not just because of God's punishment, but also as a matter
of conscience. That is also why you pay taxes, because
the authorities are working for God when they fulfill
their duties. Pay, then, what you owe them; pay them
your personal and property taxes, and show respect and
honor for them all.*

—ROMANS 13:3–7 (TEV, EMPHASIS MINE)

Twice in the above scripture civil authorities are called "God's servants," and we are charged to give them due honor and respect.
Notice also, Paul emphasizes all of them, not just some of them. I
find this strong sensation in my heart every time I see a policeman,
fireman, councilman, mayor, state legislator, governor, judge, con-

gressman, senator, or some other person in a branch of government. I find respect and honor welling up within me when I go to city, state, or federal offices. I've come to learn this is the fear of the Lord residing within my heart.

Recently I was hurrying to get to an important staff meeting. The school year started that week, and for the previous two and a half months of summer vacation I'd been able to drive thirty-five miles per hour through our neighborhood. However, when school is in session the speed limit drops to twenty miles per hour during certain hours. In rushing to get to the meeting, I didn't notice the flashing light warning drivers of the reduced speed zone, and drove through at thirty-one miles per hour. I saw the policeman on his motorcycle hidden in the bushes turn on his flashing lights, and immediately I pulled over.

He was serious and firm as most officers are when asking for a driver's license and proof of insurance. I was respectful and acknowledged my full awareness of why he pulled me over, and that I was sorry. We exchanged further dialog regarding my violation. He then commented that most people complain, make excuses, and gripe when he pulls them over.

I replied, "Sir, I'm guilty."

He said that the fine for doing this speed through a school zone is $220. But to my surprise, he handed back my license and insurance, said, "Have a nice day," and started walking back to his motorbike.

I was shocked. I called back, "Aren't you going to give me a ticket?" He just smiled and waved back. I drove away feeling a tremendous sense of mercy. To say I was grateful is an understatement.

This has not always happened. I've received a few tickets down through the years even when treating officers with the same respect. I recall a specific incident driving with a new employee to the airport. I lost sight of my speed and was pulled over, again in my own neighborhood. My assistant, thinking he was going to find favor with me, snarled a crude name coupled with a derogatory comment toward the policeman before he reached our car. He was upset at the policeman because I was going just a few miles per hour over the limit; other officers might have overlooked the offense.

Again, I was kind and respectful to this policeman, but he was not as nice or lenient as the one I described above. He was stern and proceeded to give me a ticket for the full fine. I purposefully waited until after he gave me the ticket then said, "I'm sorry, sir, for what I've done; I know I'm guilty. Thank you for doing your job and serving our community." (I knew once the ticket was recorded on his hand-held computer it couldn't be retracted.)

The officer's demeanor totally changed, and the tone of his voice lightened up. He softened when he saw my respect for his authority. He now acted as if he wanted to take back the ticket, but we both knew he couldn't. I wanted to bless this man whom I saw as a minister of God according to the book of Romans. We concluded with some friendly conversation.

Once the officer let us go, I turned to my employee and said, "If you thought you'd find favor with me by slamming the officer, you did just the opposite." I then proceeded to instruct him.

It didn't take long for him to realize his upbringing didn't foster such a respectful view of policemen and that his attitude, which he thought was normal, was completely contrary to what the Word of God instructs us in regard to civil authorities. He learned the principle of honoring civil authorities after that incident.

Civil Authority Reward

Let me share with you a testimony that highlights the reward aspect of honoring civil authorities. I began traveling in the late eighties. During my early years of travel, I spoke a few times for a church located in the Midwest. They numbered approximately one hundred and fifty and were stagnate. I went year after year, but they just hovered around the same mark. Eventually I stopped going. A few years later I received an invitation to their yearly conference (something they didn't have before). I noticed there were some well-known speakers confirmed, and they informed us their attendance would be over eight hundred. To say the least, I was surprised.

Curiosity set in. After prayer I told my assistant to accept the meeting. Again I traveled to their city and sure enough upon pulling into the parking lot of their new building I immediately noticed it was jammed with cars. Upon stepping into their auditorium I was overwhelmed by the fact of it being packed out with roughly eight to nine hundred people. The presence of God was much stronger than I ever experienced in this church before; we had a great service.

After the meeting I was alone with the pastor and questioned, "What happened? You were stagnant for years, how did the church grow so quickly? I've only been away for three years."

Without hesitation he told me the turning point. He said, "John, I got so tired of hearing my people complain about paying their taxes and how wrong our civil leaders were, I had to do something about it. So I took it to prayer and God gave me an idea."

He went to the city officials and asked about their greatest need. They shared with him that their fire department needed special masks to enable the firefighters to see through smoke. Most fire-related deaths are due to smoke inhalation, rather than burning. The problem for the fighters is often the smoke is so dense they have trouble seeing someone who is just feet in front of them. These special masks enable them to easily see the victims and quickly complete the rescue. It was the city's greatest need, but wasn't in their budget. Just one mask cost twenty-five thousand.

The pastor stepped into his pulpit the next Sunday morning and preached out of the thirteenth chapter of Romans. In love, he corrected his congregation for complaining against the city officials.

He told his people they were God's servants and that believers could not be blessed by trying to cut corners in paying their taxes and dishonoring civil leaders. Once he laid a firm scriptural foundation he proceeded to tell the city's need for the fire mask, and announced he would receive a special offering to give to the city to buy the mask. He told his congregation it was a good way to honor those whom God had appointed to serve them in a civil capacity.

The church responded by repenting of their attitude, and giving twenty-five thousand in the offering. The pastor called the mayor and asked if he could gather the city leaders that week, because his church was going to give them the money to purchase the mask. Upon arriving at City Hall the pastor and his leaders were surprised at how many officials and workers attended this presentation to witness this amazing gesture of honor.

Before presenting the check he read from Romans 13 and shared how his church members appreciated the city officials and workers, and they viewed them as ministers of God. He thanked them for all they were doing to protect and serve the people of the community. They were overwhelmed by the honor and generosity the church displayed. (Often we convey honor through financially giving. Recall, honor is to value. We will put our finances in what we value.)

Then the pastor said to me, "Several months later we held our new building dedication. Scores of city workers and officials attended. Many were saved and made the decision to attend our church. It is what blew open this community to us."

We must remember, Jesus said, "He who receives (honors) a prophet in the name of a prophet shall receive a prophet's reward." He specifically spoke of church authority, but recall that the spiritual laws of authority often span the borders to all areas of authority. So it could also be said, "He who honors civil authority in the name of civil authority shall receive the reward civil authorities carry." What is their reward? The answer is the key to the community. They are the natural gatekeepers of our towns, cities, states, and nations; and this is God given. How many communities and nations could be blown open for the entrance of the gospel if all the churches united in honoring their government leaders instead of criticizing them and attempting to get out of paying taxes?

A Makeover

I have a good friend named Danny who pastors a large church in Adelaide, Australia. Last year while preaching in his conference he shared with me a remarkable story. He came before his church and shared his desire to honor those in his city who labor to serve and protect. After considerable thought and prayer he felt the greatest need was their public high school system. So he found the most run-down high school in the city; their building and grounds were a total mess. He approached the leaders and asked if their church could come in for one Saturday and give them a huge "makeover." They happily agreed.

He went before the church and shared the vision to honor the city. He asked all the carpenters and tradesmen to donate their talents for that one day. He then asked the rest of the church to give their labor. The church leaders organized the massive undertaking over several weeks. The materials were purchased and equipment secured to make this school look brand new.

He then showed me a video of the big day. I watched carpenters rip out old trim and other rotted and beaten-up areas; workers taking out lockers and replacing them with new ones; scores of men and women sanding, taping, and painting. I watched them put up new chalkboards, install new equipment, till the grounds and lay down new sod, and plant trees, shrubs, and flowers. An overall video pan was done of the school before the work began and another immediately after the day of renovation. It simply was amazing; it looked brand new.

The church was so excited to have served the city. One thing is always certain: the joy that fills your heart when you honor those who are not expecting it. They felt their reward was the satisfaction of being able to help their city in the name of the Lord Jesus Christ. However, there was even a greater reward. The prime minster of Australia, John Howard, heard of what this church did to bless its city, and announced he would visit the church to thank them personally. I watched the video footage of the nation's leader coming to the church and expressing his heartfelt gratitude. As a result, this church is one of the most respected churches in the entire city. Its reputation and influence grew in a huge way in the community and nation.

This is not the end! Multiplied momentum was created when Pastor Danny began sharing the renovation story. In response many other churches have initiated their own projects—over two hundred schools have now been renovated all over Australia, England, Sweden, Singapore, and Malaysia.

Pastor Danny's church has also continued with their community focus by renovating the local women's prison. During the project, the church developed a working relationship with the Correctional Services Department, which resulted in prisoners being granted "day visits" to attend the church—many women are now saved and having meetings in the prison.

A Good Reputation

You may wonder why it is so important to have a good reputation with the city. The reason is simple. First of all it's scriptural. The apostle Paul states that church leaders "must have a good reputation and be well thought of by those outside [the church], lest he become involved in slander and incur reproach and fall into the devil's trap" (1 Tim. 3:7, AMP). We bring offense to the gospel by not having a good reputation among those who are outside the church; this in turn hinders the furtherance of the gospel, which is the devil's trap.

An unbeliever in Rome wrote of the Christians of the first-century church, "They pass their days on earth, but they are citizens of heaven. They obey the prescribed laws, and at the same time, they surpass the laws by their lives" (letter to Diognetus, chapter 5).

The book of Acts records this statement about the church in Jerusalem: "The people (*outside the church*) held them in high regard and praised and made much of them" (Acts 5:13, AMP, words in parentheses mine). Why did the citizens hold them in high regard? Because of their higher lifestyle. An aspect of true holiness is the ability to rise to Kingdom-level thinking and living.

Someone may ask, "But John, are we to compromise the gospel to honor and reach civil authorities?" Definitely not! John the Baptist warned Herod of his lawlessness because of sleeping with his brother's wife. In fact, it was the reason his head was removed.

I know a minister who met with President Clinton and warned of the judgment that would result in his life and the nation if he and the other leaders continued to legislate the killing of innocent children (abortion). This minister did it in such a way that the president had great respect for the warning, as did Herod with John.

Herod feared John as a prophet. So many come to officials with attitudes of superiority, criticism, and judgment—attitudes far from honor. Shadrach, Meshach, and Abed-Nego spoke with honor to the king, even though they spoke against his idolatry.

A Contrast

My wife had a dream I will never forget. During the years President Clinton was in office she woke me up one night shaken. She said, "John, I had a dream I must tell you about." (God speaks to Lisa frequently through dreams.)

She proceeded, "You and I were in a huge auditorium listening to a minister. Who the minister was, I don't know, but he was popular among Christians. He was speaking against and defaming President

Clinton. He ranted on and on of how bad he was. The majority of the congregation was enthusiastically shouting, 'Amen,' affirming what he was saying. You and I were very uncomfortable."

She continued. "Then I saw in the shadows a man get up and walk out at the rear of the large auditorium. I felt I was to follow him. As I got out into the foyer of the building he turned and glanced at me; it was President Clinton. He was overwhelmed with grief and sadness, heartbroken; then he collapsed."

She then said, "John, I knew in my dream he had come to the church for support and help. But the church was scorning him; void of true love and compassion. God was showing me that we were hardening his heart, causing him to turn from what was needed, both for him personally and the nation."

Let's compare this dream to a friend of mine who pastors a large church in western America. He also runs the National Prayer Center in our nation's capital. God has put it on his heart to minister to the Senate, House of Representatives, and other leaders in Washington. He travels to Washington, D.C., roughly twenty-two weeks a year, yet his church of thousands continues to thrive and grow.

He has shared with me, "John, I meet with these leaders to do one thing, and only one thing: to thank them for serving our country, and to ask if I can pray for them."

He's shared with me that many times he needs to instruct pastors and groups from churches how to treat government representatives when they come for a visit. Often he has to disarm their judgmental attitude toward their leaders before meeting them; they're viewed as liberal, and it blinds their eyes to the fact God says to honor and pray for these leaders.

Then he said church groups are frequently surprised by how tender and open the leaders are. It stems from the fact that the church groups have come to honor them, rather than ask for something, or give them a piece of their mind. Let me share with you two testimonies I received from him. As you read these, please understand the two leaders he is speaking of are considered to be very liberal.

I had met with this congressman a few times earlier. We had a university-age group from a church who were musicians and the congressman invited us into his office where he and a few of his staffers also met with us. We began to dialogue with him with our standard presentation. This involves us thanking him for his serving the people of his district and serving our nation so faithfully.

He then shared a few thoughts and asked us some questions.

Following this I asked him if he would mind if we sang and then prayed for him. He willingly said yes.

As we began to sing you could feel the anointing rise in the room, and soon everyone had tears in their eyes. After singing both a patriotic and gospel song, we ended with prayer. It was so impacting that when we were done no one could say anything, including the congressman.

Finally he looked at me and tried to describe in his language what he felt and how he was moved. He couldn't. He finally said: "Pastor, you know I have two young children at home. I really need to get them back to church, don't I?"

And with that he shared his thankfulness to us for coming.

Another story he shared with me of a congressman is as follows:

The first time I met with this congressman we were ushered into his office with about fifteen intercessors from a church along with their pastor. I could tell from his body language he wasn't sure what we wanted since we were a church group and represented the National Prayer Center.

He was very gracious and then asked us what he could do for us. I proceeded to tell him we were not there to receive anything from him but rather we came simply to thank him for his service to our country and then to pray for him before we left.

He then relaxed in his seat and said, "This is a gift to me." He then began to describe what he goes through every day as people come into his office and request money. He said he pictures a digital readout on the wall that adds up to all the money requested each day. He then turned to us and said, "But you have come to give me something today. That has never happened before."

We then prayed for him and as we finished up he said, "Would you mind praying for my staff as well?" So his staffers came in and we prayed for them also.

As we finished he looked at his watch and said, "I just had an appointment cancellation. Would you mind if I took you over to the Capitol and showed you around?" (This is not something a congressman does. This is reserved for interns or the lower-level staffers.)

He then proceeded to take us over to the Capitol where he led us around for about half an hour. At the end of this time the congressman and I exchanged cards and the representative left.

About two weeks later I received a frantic yet excited phone call from the pastor of this church. He began to tell me he just received a phone call from this congressman who asked if he could come to his church that weekend. We talked about how he should handle it, and sure enough that Sunday the congressman showed up with his wife and chief of staff.

After the worship service the pastor introduced him and his wife and they shared for a while. Following this they prayed for him and his wife who were greatly moved. This all happened as a result of honoring and praying for the congressman in his office.

My pastor friend has scores of testimonies just like this. You may now be questioning, "Are we to bring truth to our leaders?" Yes, just as John the Baptist did, as the minister who warned President Clinton, and others have, and still others will continue to do. However, if the church is not perceived by our leaders as those who walk in the love and compassion of Jesus Christ, and true honor for their positions of authority, they will not listen to our words. We must speak the truth, but it must be spoken in love, and in the fear of the Lord.

There will be times God will send His servant(s) to a civil leader with a strong word, such as the prophets did with the kings in the Old Testament. However, what good does it do when we are criticizing our leaders in our homes, small groups, and church services and supporting those who do the same? That is nothing more than backbiting. What we say in private we must be willing to say with a heart burning with love and honor before the face of our leaders. If not, we will poison our spirits and it will manifest in the presence of our leaders.

Honor the King

Hear the words of the apostle Peter. He says we are to, "Fear God. Honor the king" (1 Pet. 2:17).

Peter is saying, "How can you say you fear God whom you do not see, when you cannot honor the leader He has placed His authority upon that you do see?" If we fear God we will honor leaders, whether civil, social, family, or church.

As stated in the previous chapter, in America we say to a leader, "You will have to earn my respect." However, the fear of the Lord says, "I see the authority that God has placed on you, therefore you already have my respect."

I did a study of the king Peter was specifically addressing. Of course the scripture is of no private interpretation; his words are directed to all believers throughout the course of time to honor the leaders of their nation. However, in Peter's case it was Herod Agrippa I, a very corrupt and self-serving leader.

This man came into power in AD 37, after the resurrection of Jesus. He did so through cleverness and tact. With his far-seeing mind he cultivated every means that might lead to his own promotion. A key political maneuver after the Roman emperor Caligula was murdered was to help Claudius gain the throne. Claudius rewarded his shrewd political move, and he confirmed Agrippa in his ruling position and added the territories of Judea and Samaria. He became ruler of a kingdom as large as that of his grandfather, Herod the Great.

During his rule, Herod Agrippa I was forced to side in the struggle between Judaism and the Christian sect. Without hesitation he assumed the role of the Christians' bitter persecutor. We read in the New Testament, "Now about that time Herod [Agrippa I] the king stretched out his hand to harass some from the church. Then he killed James the brother of John with the sword. And because he saw that it pleased the Jews, he proceeded to further seize Peter also" (Acts 12:1–3). This ruler was cruel to believers because it served his political purposes and gained him favor with the Jews. He'd killed James, one of Jesus' three closest apostles, and he intended to kill Peter.

Agrippa's plans to execute Peter were thwarted by the prayers and obedience of the church (see vv. 5–19). This deliverance significantly strengthened the believers. The reward of their obedience is found in Scripture: "But the word of God grew and multiplied" (v. 24).

The constant prayers of the saints and their obedience to honor authority had a greater impact on the turn of events. As we continue to read, we find that Herod Agrippa I set a day in which he came before the people, sat on his throne in royal apparel, and gave a public address: "And the people kept shouting, 'The voice of a god and not of a man!' Then immediately an angel of the Lord struck him, because he did not give glory to God. And he was eaten by worms and died" (vv. 22–23).

Judgment came, but it was by the sword of the Lord, not by God's people. God is the One who brings judgment on authorities. We are commanded to pray and honor these leaders. If there is need of judgment, God says we are to make room for it. We withhold His promise to judge righteously by our disobedience to not pray and honor our leaders. So in effect we take away the very thing our nation or community needs—divine intervention.

A Modern-Day Example

This very same thing happened in recent times in the nation of Nigeria. A wicked leader, Sani Abacha, came into power in 1993 by annulling the general election and jailing its presumed winner, Moshood Abiola. He then executed many of the democratic leaders and began his dictatorial rule. Many innocent people were killed under his leadership, and approximately three billion dollars was embezzled into his own accounts in Europe.

I have a close pastor friend, Mark, who frequently travels to Nigeria. He has become friends with two leading Nigerian pastors, E. A. Abdoye and Bishop David Oyedepo, who are responsible for a huge Christian movement. Their monthly prayer meetings have a normal attendance of one million believers. Twice a year they have special prayer meetings, one in June and the other in December, both of which exceed two million people.

My friend, along with others who frequently visit this nation, tells me the believers in Nigeria respect and greatly honor their civil authorities. On the other hand, they pray diligently for their leaders and for righteousness to reign in their nation.

Pastor Mark told me in the monthly prayer meeting in early 1998, a third well-known Nigerian pastor from the north, Pastor Emmanuel Kure, saw the clouds part and two huge angels appear with giant swords. God showed him Abacha's days were now numbered; in fact he prophesied it would happen within three months. There would be no escaping if he did not repent.

Word got back to the president of what Pastor Kure spoke. So Abacha sent a "peace offering," a huge sum of money, to hopefully turn this prophecy around. Pastor Kure shared with Mark that the Lord told him, "Do not touch it, lest his [Abacha's] leprosy come upon you." Pastor Kure then sent word that he needed to repent and turn to the Lord.

God opened the door for the pastor who leads the prayer meeting, E. A. Adeboye, to speak to President Abacha. He also warned him that if he didn't repent he would be removed from office through death.

During the large prayer meeting in June 1998, three months after Kure saw the angels, Pastor Adeboye told the gathering to turn to the people around them and wish each other "Happy New Year." The audience was a bit puzzled. He told them the yoke is broken and there will be dancing in the streets.

Within twenty-four hours of this proclamation the president died unexpectedly of a heart attack. A news report read (which I obtained from the Internet), "According to the BBC, state radio quoted local news reports as saying Nigerians celebrated in the streets across the country at the news of his death." The people in the prayer meeting realized Abeboye was referring to the yoke of the dictator's rule.

At the time of this writing, Nigeria has a Christian in the office of president who looks to the two main pastors as spiritual leaders. The nation is experiencing a great move of God. In fact, evangelist Reinhard Bonnke was not permitted to enter the nation during the reign of Abacha. After his death the new president, Olusegun Obasanjo, invited Reinhard to his inauguration. While there the president reopened the nation to him.

Reinhard Bonnke's first crusade occurred in October 1999. As of October 2006 his crusades in Nigeria have recorded forty-two million people giving their lives to Jesus Christ as Savior and Lord. This is confirmed by written decision cards, and was reported to me by a friend who is an executive director of Bonnke's ministry.

The population of Nigeria in 2000 was 123,337,822. So in essence, forty-two million conversions is one-third of the entire nation! This is not counting the fruit of the nation's pastors, other evangelists, and believers who have labored in Nigeria since 1999 (it is interesting to note that Nigeria is one-fourth the population of the entire continent of Africa). I would call that an amazing harvest of souls. Recall what Scripture stated after Herod was put to death: "But the word of God grew and multiplied" (v. 24). Why was he put to death? Again, it was the saints walking in the fear of the Lord (which includes honoring their leaders) and the church praying collectively.

When God's people honor those in authority, pray for them, and walk in obedience to the Word of the Lord, we will see great outpourings of God's Spirit on our towns, cities, and nations. What are we waiting for?

CHAPTER 8

Honoring Social Leaders

Let as many as are servants under the yoke count their own masters worthy of all honor, that the name of God and the doctrine be not blasphemed.

—1 TIMOTHY 6:1 (ASV)

⌘

In this verse of scripture Paul addresses social authorities. This would include our employers, bosses, teachers, coaches, and so forth. As stated in an earlier chapter, today we would read this, "Let as many as are employees under hire count their employers or bosses worthy of all honor." Or it could read, "Let as many as are students under education count their teachers worthy of all honor." It would be the same for athletes and coaches or other types of relationships involving one submitting to another in a social setting.

Notice Paul says we are to honor social authorities so the name of God and the teaching of the gospel "be not blasphemed." The Amplified Bible states it, "so that the name of God and the teaching [about Him] may not be brought into *disrepute* and *blasphemed*" (emphasis mine). The word *disrepute* is defined as "the state of being held in low esteem by the public." The word *blaspheme* is defined as "to treat God or sacred things disrespectfully."

In putting these two words together we see that when we believers neglect to honor our employers, teachers, or other social leaders it will result in society having a low esteem for the kingdom of God; and can even lead to the point of treating God or sacred things disrespectfully.

How has our society treated the things of God disrespectfully? Prayer has been removed from our schools; the Ten Commandments have been taken out of our courtrooms; a good portion of our entertainment is offensive and even atheistic; much of our music blatantly insults God; our education system paints those who believe in creation as narrow minded and even a threat to the advancement of knowledge; and the list continues. Could we believers have added to our society's godless behavior by our lack of honor toward social authorities? According to Paul's words in the above scripture, this is exactly what happens when we fail to walk in true honor.

A Tragic Portrayal of the Gospel

I could give many examples of this, but the one that best portrays what Paul is saying occurred with me a few years ago. I boarded a plane to fly out of a major city and, due to my frequent-flyer status, was upgraded to first class. I sat next to a well-dressed businessman who was sipping on a mixed drink. I had an urge to get to know him and share the gospel, so I immediately began a conversation. There was a great rapport between us; a rapid and stimulating flow of thoughts and information ensued. To put it mildly, we hit it off.

He was very sharp, and I knew before directly asking him this man was a leader. So I inquired what he did, and he shared that he owned the second-largest taxi company in the city. I then directed the conversation along the lines of how he ran his company. After conversing on his work for quite some time, he then asked what I did. I replied, "I work for God as a minister of the gospel."

His friendly face immediately turned sour and he grunted and turned away. I was shocked. This man who had become so friendly suddenly spurned me and acted as if he wanted nothing to do with me. However, our conversation up to that point went so well that I knew I could prod. So I said in a lighthearted tone, "Wow, that sure got a reaction out of you. What's up with that?"

He turned back to me with a serious facial expression and said, "You know, I've come to like you, so I'll just tell you why I don't want anything to do with ministers or Christians."

Now I was very curious.

He said, "I had an employee. She was one of the 'born-again' types [I didn't say anything]. She would spend hours of work time preaching to many of my employees of their need to get 'saved.' Not only was she not productive, but she affected the productivity of the other workers.

"Finally she left us and took things that belonged to the company, and left me with an eight-thousand-dollar long-distance phone bill to her son who lived in Germany." (This was back in the mid-nineties when overseas phone calls were very expensive.)

I was heartbroken. Everyone in that company would now have a hard time hearing the Word of God because it was brought into disrepute by her behavior. She dishonored this owner and employees of the company by preaching when she should have been working, and by outright stealing. She should have been the most trusted employee. This is why Paul tells employees:

[Tell] bond servants to be submissive to their masters, to be pleasing and give satisfaction in every way. [Warn them] not to talk back or contradict, nor to steal by taking things of small value, but to prove themselves truly loyal and entirely reliable and faithful throughout, so that in everything they may be an ornament and do credit to the teaching [which is] from and about God our Savior.

—Titus 2:9–10 (AMP)

She discredited the very thing she preached. (What we live speaks so much louder than what we speak.) She brought reproach to the gospel. If she had done what God's Word says, honor her employer, she would have treated the business totally differently. To honor is to value, to submit, to treat as precious. Her attitude and behavior would have been completely different with an honoring heart. She would have been motivated to do a good job; and coupled with integrity, she would have furthered the gospel.

The rest of my conversation with this owner was spent apologizing for her behavior. He listened, but it wasn't much of a consolation. The damage was deep and would be very difficult to mend. It affected our conversation for the rest of the flight.

A few years later I told this story in a message I brought to a congregation. One of our financial partners later heard the story on a CD, and contacted our ministry with a request. He asked if we could get the information of the man's company and address. He had the desire to write a letter of apology and send an eight-thousand-dollar check to this employer as a testimony of the love of God.

I was so excited by this man's request to make amends and reach out to this company owner that I personally got involved. Upon contacting the company I learned the owner died of a heart attack six months earlier. Again, it was a devastating blow to my heart. I wondered if he heard what I said to him on that plane, but to be honest, I really couldn't get anywhere in sharing the gospel as he had a closed spirit. I could only hope another laborer came across his path and reached him. I wondered for quite some time *if he had made peace with God through Jesus Christ.* I knew it would take a miracle because of what this former employee had done.

How much easier it would have been to share the gospel with this businessowner on the plane if he would have had an employee who honored him and his company. In fact, he would have been receptive. Why? He would have said, "John, I can see what you are saying. My greatest employees have been Christians. My life is a mess. I need Jesus to give me eternal life. Yes, I want to pray with you."

On the positive side I've listened to unbelievers who are bosses report to me how they see the evidence of true Christianity in their employees, not because they preach, but because they display Christ's character in difficult situations and in their work ethic. They've reported to me, "They work harder than the other employees," or "They are the most honest and trustworthy employees I have," or "They never argue, complain, or talk back to me."

What gives these believers the ability to work so differently than the woman described above? The answer is simply the fear of the Lord, which produces true honor in our hearts for those whom God cares about and loves.

In the Classroom

I've heard scores of reports and stories down though the years of how believers have brought either credit or disrepute to the gospel through honor or dishonor in secular settings. My first encounter of witnessing this from both ends occurred while still in school.

I received Jesus Christ as my Lord in my fraternity while attending Purdue University. I was raised a Catholic and attended church faithfully, but was in great need of salvation. I recall how my fraternity brother got my attention. First off, I observed his loving but strong character and behavior. He was an amazing athlete, very disciplined in his life. I noticed at the fraternity parties he would attend only at the beginning, before the rest of us got plastered drunk, then leave when things got out of hand. While at the parties, he would converse in such a kind matter to either the guys or the girls, all the while drinking a soda.

He saw I was religious, but far from God. So he first befriended me, and after some time, one evening, he knocked on my door. In the course of sharing the Word of God with me he asked, "John, can you tell me about the president of the United States?"

I responded, "Sure, his name is Jimmy Carter, his wife's name is Roslyn. He was the former governor of Georgia, and prior to that he was a peanut farmer."

He said, "Good. Can you now tell me about Jesus Christ?"

I said, "Sure, He was born of a virgin, His stepfather was named Joseph, He had twelve disciples, and He died on a cross."

He said, "Great. Now tell me this, do you know President Carter like you know your mother?"

I quickly responded, "No."

He asked what was the difference.

I said, "She's my mom. I know her personally. I've never met the president of the United States."

He then said, "So you have a personal relationship with your mom, but even though you know much about the president, you don't know him; you don't have a personal relationship with him."

I answered, "Correct."

He then said, "Do you know Jesus Christ like you know your mother?"

I was stunned. I sat there not knowing what to say. He then showed me God's whole plan of sending Jesus was not to make us a bunch of churchgoers, but to have personal relationship with us because He longed for and loved us. I was overwhelmed to discover why I was created.

For the next year I spent hours in the Bible. I couldn't get enough. I wanted to know God's Word. Before giving my life to Jesus the Bible read as a bunch of stories and rules. Now it was God's word to me personally because it had come alive in my heart.

As an engineering student I could take a few electives. Included in the list were some courses offered through Notre Dame, which had a resident professor on Purdue's campus. I decided to take Old

Testament Survey 101. As a young believer I was struggling with understanding some of the teachings of the Old Testament, and I thought it would be great to get an overall perspective.

Our class met for three hours every Monday. The professor came before us in the first class and basically shocked me. He said there were over six hundred contradictions in the Scriptures, you could not historically prove from the Bible that Jesus Christ was raised from the dead, and when Moses crossed the Red Sea with the children of Israel, it was at that time a marsh. The reason for the Bible making it more dramatic was as the story was passed down through the generations it was exaggerated more and more, till it turned out to be a huge sea.

Needless to say I was in for a rough ride that semester. I recall many confrontational discussions with this professor and other students. During one class, the professor and I had a debate lasting two of the three hours. The whole time I spoke to him I did so with firm resolve, but stayed respectful to his position of being teacher.

We were assigned a huge research paper at the beginning of the term that was due toward the end of the semester. It was worth a third of our final grade. I'd diligently worked on the paper. In our last class the professor passed back to us the graded research papers. Upon receiving mine there was no grade on it, but rather a huge mark of "I." I was puzzled to say the least. I approached him at the end of class and he said, "John, I need you to come into my office and meet with me about the score I gave you."

A few days later I met with him in his office. He started the meeting out by saying, "John, you and I are in two different worlds. Therefore I felt I couldn't grade your research paper. So I put an 'I' on it, and that basically means it will not count toward your final grade. So what I'm doing with you is averaging your two exams for your final grade for the semester."

He then said, "John, I've had a number of 'fundamentalists' in my class and they've been some of my biggest headaches. Most all of them have done one of three things: they create havoc for my class, they drop out of the class, or some have even backed down from their beliefs."

He softened and said, "John, you've been different. You've not backed down from your beliefs one bit. You've stood your ground, and yet you've spoken to me in a respectful way. You've also earned the respect of your fellow classmates. I'm very grateful for your courage and the respect you've shown me."

God showed me something through our conversation. When we stand firm in the revelation of His Word, but do it in a way that honors our leaders, we will see God move on the behalf of truth. The other "fundamentalists" he had in his class were most likely born-again believers. Yet their witness in that class was just the opposite of what they were attempting to do: communicating Jesus Christ to their fellow classmates and this teacher. It would appear they brought disrepute to the true gospel in the eyes of the teacher and classmates by their contentious and disrespectful behavior, which created havoc in this man's class. A great opportunity was missed because of not walking in the honor principle.

We are never to back down from what God's Word states. We are to stand firm. However, we are to correct those who are in opposition with a meek and gentle spirit. If it is our bosses, coaches, or teachers, we are to live a Christlike example. If the opportunity arises, then we are to open our mouths and speak the truth with love and respect to our leaders.

Honoring Social Authorities

How do we honor social authorities? Let's again look at the meaning of honor. It is to value, to treat as precious and weighty, to treat with deference, to submit, and to obey as long as it doesn't contradict Scripture.

If we meditate and take this definition to prayer, our behavior will positively affect our workplaces, classrooms, or playing fields. If we ask God to fill our hearts with honor toward our social authorities, we will treat them accordingly. Instead of fighting for our rights, we will prefer their desires to our own. We will seek to make them successful whether or not we are recognized, or properly paid for our labor. How can we do this? Scripture tells us,

> Slaves (*employees*), obey your earthly masters (*employers or bosses*) with deep respect and fear. Serve them sincerely as you would serve Christ. Work hard, but not just to please your masters when they are watching. As slaves of Christ, do the will of God with all your heart. Work with enthusiasm, as though you were working for the Lord rather than for people. Remember that the Lord will reward each one of us for the good we do.
>
> —Ephesians 6:5–8 (NLT, words in parentheses mine)

Notice the statement "Work with enthusiasm, as though you were working for the Lord." If this is in our hearts we will move from being slaves to servants. You may say, "I'm not a slave." Before you quickly respond to this statement, let me tell you the difference between a slave and a servant. A slave does the minimum requirement; the servant does the maximum potential. A slave is stolen from, a servant gives; a slave has to, the servant gets to. The servant looks for opportunities, rather than waits for orders. He foresees the needs of the one he serves and fills them without having to be asked.

If you think your boss is treating you unfairly and is hard on you, you need to act and not react. The person who reacts complains of how he's mistreated, or mopes and is unproductive. The person who acts will attack evil with good (see Rom. 12:21). He will approach the boss who is unkind to him and say something like, "Sir, I see there is some extra work that needs to be done, so I want you to know that I'm going to come in two hours early for the next week and get this done and you don't need to pay me a thing extra for it."

If you address conflict in this manner, you will win the favor of God and eventually man. How do I know this? Proverbs 3:3–4 tells us when we write mercy and truth on the tablets of our hearts we will "find favor and high esteem in the sight of God and man."

If you don't find favor in the eyes of your boss with this type of honoring behavior, God will open a door in another place where you will find this favor, as did the insurance executive we discussed in a previous chapter. He honored his employer even when they dishonored him. God eventually opened the door for him in a larger company and he is now walking in a full reward as one of their top executives.

It is a law. If you honor the social authorities in your life, God will honor you, and you will be fully rewarded. It may not come from your boss, teacher, or coach, but it will come. God is watching over His Word to perform it!

CHAPTER 9

Honoring Domestic Leaders

∝

Let's turn our attention to the family. We'll start out by discussing children. Scripture tells us, " 'Honor your father and mother,' which is the first commandment with promise: 'that it may be well with you and you may live long on the earth' " (Eph. 6:2–3).

To honor our parents is not a suggestion, nor a recommendation; rather it's a commandment. Have some forgotten we're to keep the commandments of God as New Testament believers? It's evidence the love of God truly abides in us. Jesus says, "He who has My commandments and keeps them, it is he who loves Me" (John 14:21). John the apostle confirms by writing, "This is love, that we walk according to His commandments" (2 John 6).

Once we receive Jesus Christ as Lord we are changed; the person who previously existed no longer lives. We are literally a new creation. Our hearts are made new with the fear and love of God residing in us. Our desires now are toward God; we long to please Him, for that is in our nature. We'll live in such a way that "keeping the commandments of God is what matters" (1 Cor. 7:19).

Conversely, those who habitually ignore God's commandments haven't had a genuine encounter with Jesus Christ through the Holy Spirit. They may confess Christianity, but as Jesus instructs, we'll know their true nature by their lifestyle (see Matt. 7:20). If they disregard or take the commandments of God lightly, they do not have His heart. John writes, "He who says, 'I know Him (*Jesus Christ*),' and does not keep His commandments, is a liar (*deceived*), and the truth is not in him" (1 John 2:4, words in parentheses mine). John clearly tells us this person is not a child of God; he is deceived. He may think he is saved, but in reality he's not.

Let's again recap the meaning of honor: to value, to esteem, to respect, to treat favorably, to have high regard for. In viewing our parents through the eyes of honor we will communicate with them in respect and love. Recall honor can be displayed in deed, word, and even thought, but all true honor originates from the heart. So if young men or women speak in a flippant, careless, or irreverent way on a regular basis to their parents, they are displaying outwardly their lack of true honor for their parents. For out of the abundance of the heart the mouth speaks (see Matt. 12:34). Their dishonor can also be displayed by their behavior, such as by the tone of voice, rolling eyes, disgusted look, dragging feet to carry out a request, complaining, and so forth.

Dishonoring our parents has become a normal way of life in America. It's steeped in our culture. There are a number of popular "family movies" that I couldn't permit my children to watch. Some are even rated "G," and put out by "trusted film companies." We would normally consider them safe. The story lines are often touching. However, the manner in which the children converse with their parents is a totally different story. They treat their father or mother as stupid and out of touch. They blatantly disregard their parents' directives, and the movie concludes with the children winding up as the heroes, or they would get their heart's desire, even though they treated their parents with contempt. You may think I've gone too far, but hear what God says: "Cursed is he who dishonors his father or his mother. All the people shall say, Amen" (Deut. 27:16, AMP).

Wow, do you understand how strong the word *cursed* is? To be cursed by God is a very serious issue. We may expect to hear, "Cursed is he who murders, steals, practices sexual immorality, or witchcraft." Yet God says the one who dishonors his father or mother is cursed. Let's go over again the meaning of the word *dishonor:* to treat as common, ordinary, or menial. A stronger version of it is to treat shamefully, or to humiliate.

A Curse That Lasted Generations

There are a number of examples in Scripture how men brought curses on their lives by dishonoring parents. One, which is vivid, is Noah's youngest son, Ham.

After the flood, Noah took up farming. One evening he drank himself drunk. Why would he do this? Perhaps he fought feelings of depression, since he was the last dad on the face of the earth; or maybe he sought relief from the pressures of rebuilding after the flood. In either case he obviously was overwhelmed with pressure and sought relief, but through the wrong means. Once inebriated, he stumbled into his tent, took off all his clothes, and passed out.

Ham entered the tent where his dad lay, observed his naked body, gasped, and went out and told everybody (there weren't a whole lot of men to tell at this time, just Shem and Japheth). I can just see him giggling, and with a sneer in his voice saying, "Hey guys, you're not going to believe this; Dad is drunk as a skunk and naked as a jay-bird! You gotta see this, come on."

When Shem and Japheth heard their brother's derisive report, they responded differently. They grabbed a garment, held it over their shoulders while walking into the tent backward, and covered Noah's nakedness. They didn't want to see the shame of their father.

The next morning Noah woke up and discovered what Ham did. We read:

> Then he cursed the descendants of Canaan, the son of Ham;
> "A curse on the Canaanites! May they be the lowest of ser-

vants to the descendants of Shem and Japheth." Then Noah said, "May Shem be blessed by the LORD my God; and may Canaan be his servant. May God enlarge the territory of Japheth, and may he share the prosperity of Shem; and let Canaan be his servant."

—Genesis 9:25–27 (NLT)

This prophetic word from Noah's mouth was played out for several generations. The Canaanites, who were the descendants of Ham, were cursed and eventually overtaken by the children of Israel at God's command.

Ham dishonored his father and brought a curse upon his life and descendants. It is interesting to note that Ham's behavior brought severe consequence to him, while Noah's drunkenness brought none recorded in Scripture. In fact, Hebrews 11 says that God boasts of the patriarchs. One of them is Noah—oh yes, the man who was falling-down drunk. It is obvious he repented of his sin and was forgiven. However, you don't read about Ham in that chapter; in fact, you never hear his name mentioned again in the Bible in a positive light.

The moral failure of Noah became a test of honor to his three sons; it revealed their hearts. One lacked honor and was rebellious; the other two were respectful and refrained from judging what they were not responsible for. Noah's behavior was not godly, but it was God's to deal with, definitely not the son's. The two who understood this could continue to honor him from their hearts; the one son who took it upon himself to judge his father's actions fell into dishonor and consequently became cursed.

Another very interesting fact to note is that Ham was accurate in his report. His father was drunk and naked, yet Ham was wrong in principle. Logic would justify his actions: he repeated only what he saw; he was only being "truthful." Yet the principle of honor and Kingdom authority says otherwise.

Dishonor Grows over Time

Another man who dishonored his father in Scripture was Reuben. He was Jacob's firstborn; his mother was Leah. How did Reuben dishonor his father? By sleeping with one of his father's concubines, Bilhah.

However, I believe there was a little more to this than just having sex with one who belonged to his father. There were two primary wives of Jacob, Leah and Rachel, who were also sisters. Bilhah was Rachel's maid. Rachel and Leah were in competition with each other. The rivalry ignited and grew stronger, due to Jacob favoring Rachel. He did this from the start of their marriage, and it continued until Rachel's death.

When God saw that Leah was unloved by her husband, and He opened her womb, she conceived and bore Reuben. Her response at the birth of Reuben was, "The LORD has surely looked on my affliction. Now therefore, my husband will love me" (Gen. 29:32).

After a while she birthed a second son. At his birth she said, " 'Because the LORD has heard that I am unloved, He has therefore given me this son also.' And she called his name Simeon (*means "heard"*)" (v. 33, words in italics are mine).

A third time she bore a son. Her growing desperation is shown by what she said at his birth: " 'Now this time my husband will become attached to me, because I have borne him three sons.' Therefore his name was called Levi (*means "attached"*)" (v. 34, words in italics are mine).

When Rachel saw the prosperity of her sister and that she couldn't get pregnant, she devised a plan to thwart any ground Leah may have been gaining on her. She would give Jacob her maid, so she said, "Here is my maid Bilhah; go in to her, and she will bear a child on my knees, that I also may have children by her" (30:3). Once the baby was born, Rachel said, "With great wrestlings I have wrestled with my sister, and indeed I have prevailed" (v. 8).

Reuben, being the firstborn, witnessed all the strife and contention between his mother and Rachel. He was old enough to see the pain of his own mother being ignored by his father. So it happened Reuben went into the fields and found mandrakes for his mother. Once Leah received them from her son, Rachel became envious and desired the mandrakes, so a bargain was struck. Rachel would give Leah a night to sleep with Jacob.

When Jacob came out of the field that night, Leah met him and said, "You must come in to me, for I have surely hired you with my son's mandrakes" (v. 16). It is evident from this incident Jacob spent most of his nights sleeping with Rachel, and the only way Leah could secure him was by paying for it.

Reuben painfully observed all these harsh dealings within his family. I'm sure his resentment of his father's unfavorable and un-kind behavior toward his mother was growing stronger by the day.

It didn't stop with just bedroom activity. It was seen in all areas. Time passed, and after ten sons were born to Jacob, finally Rachel had a child, Joseph. Reuben's resentment multiplied, observing how his father favored the only son of Rachel. Joseph was given preferen-tial treatment, was loved more than all the other brothers, and was even given a glorious robe signifying his father's preference.

When the family fled from Laban, Leah's and Rachel's father, word came to them Esau was on the move traveling to meet the family with four hundred men. Fear seized Jacob, because he well remembered his brother's vow to kill him for stealing his birthright.

Jacob, in an attempt to salvage his life and posterity, divided his family. He sent them in groups before him to meet Esau. The thought was, if Esau killed the first groups, Jacob could flee from his brother in time to save his life and those closest to him. Let's look at how he divided his family: "And he put the maids and their children in front, Leah and her children after them, and Rachel and Joseph last of all" (33:2, AMP). Can you imagine the hurt or anger felt by Reuben? He and his mother are put out in front of Rachel to die, while his father favors Rachel and her son and places them in his last group with Jacob.

Time continued to pass; resentment continued to grow. Rachel gave birth to a second son and died in the process. Jacob mourned greatly and set a pillar on her grave, which would remain for generations to come. It's interesting to note, you never hear of Leah's pillar, only Rachel's. So it is obvious this grave monument was huge and glorious. Most likely, by now Reuben was fuming with bitterness.

The Bible reads immediately after the death of Rachel, "Reuben went and lay with Bilhah" (35:22). Reuben lived in agony seeing this rivalry growing up. He resented the fact that his father favored Rachel and didn't love his own mother. It is quite possible, actually probable, that he slept with Bilhah not just to have sex but to bring shame to Rachel's tent and pay back a little of the hurt he suffered from his father's actions.

Now see what God speaks about Reuben long after all the brothers were dead and gone: "The oldest son of Israel was Reuben. But since he *dishonored* his father by sleeping with one of his father's concubines, his birthright was given to the sons of his brother Joseph. For this reason, Reuben is not listed in the genealogy as the firstborn" (1 Chron. 5:1, NLT, emphasis mine).

It's most interesting to note that Jacob's actions were wrong, in that he loved Rachel to the neglect of Leah. In fact, it was not good in the eyes of God, for we read, "When the LORD saw that Leah was unloved, He opened her womb" (Gen. 29:31). The Amplified Bible states, "When the Lord saw that Leah was despised," God blessed Leah in the area of her affliction created by her husband.

Reuben saw accurately. His assessment of his father's behavior wasn't made up. However, what he allowed to foster in his heart was what poisoned him. He let go of the honor God places in each child's heart, and embraced an attitude of resentment that fostered dishonor. He permitted it to grow to the point where he justified his dishonorable behavior toward his father. It cost him dearly. He lost his birthright.

Recall from an earlier chapter, Hannah was insulted by the priest Eli, yet she would not allow his dishonorable behavior to thwart the honor God commands us to give those in authority. She received a full reward. Reuben, on the other hand, lost his reward—his heritage. He was 100 percent right in his assessment, but he was 100 percent wrong in his response.

Don't Allow Someone Else's Wrong Behavior to Affect You

It has become increasingly clear to me in the past several years we cannot allow wrong behavior of others affect what we know to be right behavior. This truth is seen vividly in the life of Moses.

The children of Israel, just as Jacob, had consistently behaved in such a way that was not pleasing to God. With Jacob it was despising his wife; with them it was constant complaining. As with Reuben, Moses suffered from their wrong behavior. For forty years, he was denied the Promised Land and stuck in the wilderness because of what they did.

Now they were complaining again because they didn't have any water. So God told Moses to speak to a rock and then water would come out of it. But at this point, Moses was so fed up with their behavior that he gathered the Israelites and yelled out, "'Hear now, you rebels! Must we bring water for you out of this rock?' Then Moses lifted his hand and struck the rock twice with his rod" (Num. 20:10–11).

Moses' behavior resulted in him being denied the privilege of bringing the nation into the Promised Land. Years later hear what the psalmist wrote: "They angered Him also at the waters of strife, so that it went ill with Moses on account of them; because they rebelled against His Spirit, so that he spoke rashly with his lips" (Ps. 106:32–33).

Their bad behavior got to Moses. So he acted out of line with the

Word of God. It cost him dearly! I have personally written in my Bible near this verse, "We cannot blame our wrong behavior on the bad behavior of others." That is a hard lesson for each of us to learn.

Reuben's father's behavior was not honorable toward his mother, yet it didn't justify Reuben's dishonorable attitude and behavior toward his father. God tells us to honor our father and mother, regardless of how good or bad they are in our eyes, or how honorable or dishonorable their behavior is.

Again, as a very important side note, let me remind you of the important principle taught in a previous chapter. We're to always honor and submit to authority; we're to obey authority as well; however, in regard to obedience, we're not to obey an authority if they order us to do something contrary to the Word of God. An example may be if a parent tells a child to lie to their teacher, the child can respectfully say to their parent, "Mom or Dad, I respect and honor you, but I cannot lie, for that is a sin against God." Or a more severe case would be if a father is sexually assaulting a young person, the son or daughter is to seek out help from other authorities. They do not dishonor their father by seeking to get both him and themselves help.

Twofold Reward

Let's look again at our opening scripture: " 'Honor your father and mother,' which is the first commandment with promise: 'that it may be well with you and you may live long on the earth' " (Eph. 6:2–3).

The reward of honor is twofold and clearly spelled out in this verse. First, it will go well with you. You will experience success in life, along with peace, joy, love, and health. You will enjoy a rewarding life. Secondly, you will live a long life on the earth. You are promised not to die prematurely of some fatal disease, car wreck, or other unforeseen accident.

You may think, *But I know someone who honored their parents but died at a young age.* This may be true. So now you may ask, "Then why didn't this promise apply to them?" Simply put, the promises of God are not automatic; they must be acquired by faith. You may be shocked by this statement, but allow me to exemplify this truth from Scripture.

God gave a covenant promise to Abraham that through his son Isaac the promised Seed would come. The specific Word from God was, "I will establish My covenant with him for an everlasting covenant, and with his descendants after him" (Gen. 17:19). To confirm; we again read, "Your descendants will be called and counted through the line of Isaac" (Rom. 9:7, AMP). This being the case, Isaac definitely had to have children, correct?

Who picked out Isaac's wife? The answer is God Himself. Recall Abraham's servant went to look for Isaac's wife among Abraham's relatives. Upon arrival he prayed,

> "O LORD God of my master Abraham, please give me success this day, and show kindness to my master Abraham. Behold, here I stand by the well of water, and the daughters of the men of the city are coming out to draw water. Now let it be that the young woman to whom I say, 'Please let down your pitcher that I may drink,' and she says, 'Drink, and I will also give your camels a drink'—let her be the one You have *appointed* for Your servant Isaac."
>
> —Genesis 24:12–14 (emphasis mine)

Indeed, a very specific prayer; there's hardly a chance of a coincidental occurrence. These camels drink huge amounts of water, and very few strangers would be so gracious to draw that much water unless they were moved by God to do it. Abraham's servant had to be sure, so he made his request precise and difficult. Also notice he said the one who performed this task would be the *appointed* one; in other words, she was God's selected wife for Isaac.

Before he was finished speaking his prayer request, Rebekah, a daughter of Abraham's relatives, came out with a pitcher on her shoulder. Abraham's servant hurried over and entreated her: "Please let me drink a little water from your pitcher" (v. 17). Notice he made no mention of the camels. He asked her exactly as he made the request in prayer. She gladly agreed and gave him some water. Now read what happens next: "And when she had finished giving him a drink, she said, 'I will draw water for your camels also, until they have finished drinking'" (v. 19).

It happened exactly as Abraham's servant requested. He was amazed and overwhelmed with joy. He delighted in how quickly his prayer was answered.

However, the job wasn't complete. Now the final bridge of God's confirmed choice for Isaac had to be crossed. Would her family allow her to leave with a man they'd never met and be taken permanently to a land they weren't familiar with?

Once Abraham's servant recited the story to Rebekah's family, the men of the household answered, "The thing comes from the LORD; we cannot speak to you either bad or good" (v. 50). The following day the family permitted her to depart, and Abraham's servant brought her to Isaac, and they were wed.

Now here is the amazing part of the story. God picked out this woman for Isaac miraculously. However, once they were married it was discovered that Rebekah was barren; she could not have children. What! Why would God pick out a barren woman for Isaac, when He promised the Seed would come through Isaac? The answer lies in the fact that promises of God are not automatic; they have to be acquired and received by faith. We read, "Now Isaac pleaded with the LORD for his wife, because she was barren; and the LORD granted his plea, and Rebekah his wife conceived" (Gen. 25:21).

The Amplified Bible says, "Isaac prayed much to the Lord for his wife because she was unable to bear children; and the Lord granted his prayer, and Rebekah his wife became pregnant." What was he praying? He cried out, "God, You promised that nations and kings would come through me, and the Seed would come through my descendants. How can this happen if my wife is unable to have children? I pray, oh Lord, open Rebekah's womb that the promised Seed may come forth according to Your promise."

A Spiritual Law

There is a spiritual law we must know and understand. Scripture makes this declaration: "Forever, O LORD, Your word is settled in heaven" (Ps. 119:89).

Notice it does *not* say, "Forever Your word is settled in heaven and earth." No, it clearly states His word is forever established in heaven; nothing is said about the earth. How then is His word established in the earth? In further examining of the Scriptures we are told, "By the *mouth* of two or three witnesses *every word shall be established*" (2 Cor. 13:1, emphasis mine). Notice it is out of the *mouth* of two, or even three, that words are established. Now see what God says: "So shall My word be that goes forth from My *mouth*; it shall *not return to Me void*, but it shall accomplish what I please, and it shall prosper in the thing for which I sent it" (Isa. 55:11, emphasis mine).

How does His word return to Him? The answer is simple—out of our mouths. God is the first; we are the second. So when we speak out of our own mouths His word that has already gone out of His mouth, we then establish it on this earth! Do you see this amazing truth? God promised through Isaac the Seed would be called, but it took Isaac speaking it out of his mouth to establish it on this earth, both in his life along with his family's.

God says if we honor our parents He promises a long life. If we speak this promise *in faith*, we establish what He has already spoken in our own lives. We are the second mouth, which establishes it here on the earth. I'm so excited right now I can hardly stand it! This means we can look disease straight in the face and declare God's covenant promise of living a long life, and it will have to flee. We can confidently speak safety in our travels, home, or anywhere else danger lurks. We can confidently say, "I will not be afraid of ten thousands of people who have set themselves against me all around" (Ps. 3:6), for with long life God will satisfy me, and show me His salvation (see Ps. 91:16).

We can also speak the promise of it going well with us. If we are facing difficulty, situations that appear to be bleak and hopeless, we can boldly say, "I've honored my mother and father, God's covenant promise to me is that it will go well with me! In Jesus' name I command the walls of lack, strife, depression, ill circumstances [and so forth] to back off and give way."

We can do this with any covenant promise of God. The only difference between those who walk in abundant life and those who suffer lack is what we've spoken out of our mouths. God says, "I call heaven and earth to witness this day against you that I have set before you life and death, the blessings and the curses; therefore choose life, that you and your descendants may live" (Deut. 30:19, AMP). Notice we are to choose life. Why? Because if we don't choose life (the covenant blessings), death is already in operation in the earth. How then do we choose life? Again we read, "Death and life are in the power of the tongue, and they who indulge in it shall eat the fruit of it" (Prov. 18:21, AMP).

We can agree either with God's covenant promises or Satan's curses of lack, sickness, and death. It's so simple many stumble over this truth. For this reason James states,

> We all make many mistakes, but those who control their tongues can also control themselves in every other way. We can make a large horse turn around and go wherever we want by means of a small bit in its mouth. . . . So also, the

tongue is a small thing, but what enormous damage it can do. A tiny spark can set a great forest on fire.

—James 3:2–3, 5 (NLT)

A tiny spark can burn down an entire forest. So words spoken in fear can bring destruction to your life. The good news is we have God's covenant promises; once we get them into our hearts, our mouths will speak accordingly. James goes on to say the tongue is like fountain of water; it cannot bring forth both fresh and bitter water at the same time. The key is not the fountain, but the earth, the source of the water. Even so, it's not the tongue, but the source— that is, what's in our hearts. For Jesus states, "Out of the abundance of the heart his mouth speaks" (Luke 6:45).

God says you'll have a good and long life if you honor your parents. As you read these words, the Holy Spirit is planting this truth in your heart, and you will begin to speak accordingly. Don't base your faith in God upon others' experiences, rather the integrity of the Word of God. I know I won't die prematurely; this promise is rooted deeply in my heart, and God is watching over His word to perform it.

The Wife's Call to Honor

In regard to the wife's role we read, "Let the wife see that she respects and reverences her husband [that she notices him, regards him, honors him, prefers him, venerates, and esteems him; and that she defers to him, praises him, and loves and admires him exceedingly]" (Eph. 5:33, AMP).

Wow, that is a mouthful! You can see Paul elaborately spells out the wife is to honor her own husband. (Later in the book I will focus on husbands honoring their wives, but in this chapter we are specifically speaking of those in authority over us.)

The husband is the head of the home. Chauvinistic men didn't conjure this up; it is God's idea. It is impossible to have true peace and blessing in a home where a wife leads or dominates, where the husband is not respected as the head. On the contrary, when a woman of God values her husband as the leader of the home, she will receive the reward of honor. It may come directly through him, but sometimes it can come by other avenues.

Recently I was ministering in a very large church in Europe. A woman said to me, "John, you are the reason I'm in this church."

I was a bit puzzled. She then told her story. Years ago the church went through a transition of leadership. She and her husband traveled a good distance to attend, so it seemed a good time to try other churches closer to their home. After visiting several, she liked a small church close to their neighborhood. However, the husband felt it wasn't the place they should join; his feeling was they should return to their original church. She did so reluctantly, but continued to go to the small church Sunday evenings.

She became more attached to and involved with the small church. Eventually the leaders of the smaller church challenged her, "When are you going to stand up to your husband and tell him you have to obey God's leading to come to our church?" (This type of leadership horrifies me.)

Their words swayed her. She told her husband of her decision to switch churches; then she made an appointment with the pastor of the original church to inform him that she would leave even though her husband would still attend. The night before the meeting she got hold of my book *Under Cover*, in which I discuss the importance of submission to authority.

She said to me, "John, I stayed up the entire night reading it. I cried through the whole book; realizing my rebellion toward God and my husband. The following day I repented to both my husband and pastor."

She willingly returned to the church. After a few months the pastor's wife introduced her to a woman in the church. It turned out they both had a similar vision for a business venture, so they began the business. Today they are very successful and are putting a good amount of finances from their business into the kingdom of God.

She said, "John, had I stayed at the other church I would have eventually left my husband and never entered into the call of business that's on my life." She further shared that the small church whose leaders persuaded her to disregard her husband's leadership no longer existed. She honored her husband, which resulted in both protection and reward.

Wives with Unsaved Husbands

The apostle Peter writes in the same way as Paul,

> You married women, be submissive to your own husbands [subordinate yourselves as being secondary to and dependent on them, and adapt yourselves to them], so that even if any do not obey the Word [of God], they may be won over not by discussion but by the [godly] lives of their wives, when they observe the pure *and* modest way in which you conduct yourselves, together with your reverence [for your husband; you are to feel for him all that reverence includes: to respect, defer to, revere him—to honor, esteem, appreciate, prize, and, in the human sense, to adore him, that is, to admire, praise, be devoted to, deeply love, and enjoy your husband].
>
> —1 Peter 3:1–2 (AMP)

Peter shows that even if the wife's husband is not saved, it is her honoring behavior that will reach him, not her preaching or teaching. I know men who've been won over to the Lord by this very conduct of their wives. A great example is Smith Wigglesworth, one of the greatest men of God in Europe in the early 1900s.

Wigglesworth was a plumber and had over time grown very cold toward God. He didn't want anything to do with Christianity. Polly, his wife, on the other hand, was a very devout believer. In fact, her zeal for God was increasing all the while. Her devotion made Wigglesworth's laxity more and more apparent and he became irritated by her presence.

He harshly persecuted her for her faith and, in no uncertain terms, told her not to go to church. She didn't adhere to his command for it was contrary to the will of God (again, as stated earlier, we are to obey authority as long as they do not tell us to violate the written Word of God).

She would make his dinner and leave for Sunday evening church. One night she came home from church later than usual. Upon entering the house Smith demanded, "I am the master of this house, and I'm not going to have you coming home at so late an hour as this!"

Polly quietly replied, "I know that you are my husband, but Christ is my Master."

Greatly annoyed and enraged, Wigglesworth opened the back door and forced her out of the house, locking the door behind her.

As it turned out, Polly's determination to obey God and honor her husband had a profound effect on Wigglesworth. He eventually came under great conviction and surrendered completely to the service of Jesus Christ, and his work is still respected and talked about to this day. Many were saved, healed, and even raised from the dead through his ministry.

Polly's reward at the judgment seat of Christ was enormous because of all the hundreds of thousands of people who have been impacted by his ministry. She received not only the reward of a changed husband but also a great harvest in the life to come.

Is it becoming clear yet? We are instructed to honor not just for the sake of those we honor, but for us as well. We personally lose if we withhold honor from whom honor is due.

CHAPTER 10

Honoring Church Leaders

⤞

As stated earlier, the kingdom of God is just that, a kingdom. Therefore within the church there will be appointed authority and order of rank. In honoring a church leader we in turn honor Jesus, and in honoring Jesus we honor God the Father (Matt. 10:40–41). How we act toward, speak to, and even think of a leader is the way we treat the One who sent the leader.

God then says, "Those who honor Me I will honor, and those who despise Me shall be lightly esteemed" (1 Sam. 2:30). Our attitude toward God is reflected by our behavior toward church leaders. You cannot say you fear God if you don't have respect for church authority.

"I Fear God, Not Man!"

I'll never forget an encounter in a service that vividly portrays this truth. After teaching on the importance of being free from offense, a large number of people responded to my call to come forward for prayer. In this large group a young man stood out who I perceived had a great amount of hurt in his life. I called him up to the platform for further ministry. When he walked up, another man slipped out of the crowd and came up and stood on the platform with us.

He had a long ponytail and was dressed in jeans, a black leather vest, and T-shirt, with tattoos running up and down his arms. He had a wild look in his eyes and was definitely on edge. I noticed the first young man instantly tensed up and was no longer free to receive.

I turned to the second man and politely asked for him to step back down off the platform.

He glared at me and roughly said, "No!"

After the initial shock of his blatant disregard of my request, I mentally regrouped and said, "Sir, I will not continue until you step down."

He again said, "No!"

I was now slightly frustrated, questioning in my mind why the ushers weren't helping me to move this man off the platform. It then occurred to me they were all terrified of him. Now fully aware I was dealing with a rebellious man with no regard for authority, I had to be firm, stay in my authority, and trust God. Knowing I couldn't reach this young man the way things were progressing, I persisted, "Sir, I am now ordering you to step down from this platform."

He glared again and said, "No!" After an awkward pause he blurted out, "I fear God, not man!"

This man did not fear God. He feared an image of God, one he made up in his own mind and heart that was not the true God of heaven and earth. If he truly feared God, he would honor me as a servant of God and submit to my request.

I wouldn't relent, so I looked inside for the Holy Spirit's help. Suddenly, as if someone told me, I simply knew this man was the boy's father. So I asked and he affirmed he indeed was. I said, "Sir, if you want your son to receive help from God, you need to step off the platform; if not, you will be responsible for withholding God's healing power from your son."

These words seemed to penetrate his hardness, enough that he reluctantly stepped down from the platform; still with a glaring stare focused on me. The son eventually opened back up to receive ministry and was powerfully touched by God. It was truly amazing what God did in him. He broke and sobbed.

After the service I met with the father in the pastor's office. He was a member of a rough motorcycle gang in the city. He was tough and appeared unreachable, but I wouldn't back off. Though I spoke gently with him, our confrontation became so intense, I thought at one point he would attack me physically.

I told him it was impossible to fear God and have no regard for His servants. To fear God is to respect the authorities He appoints. I shared with him why it was wrong for him to refuse my request for him to step off the platform.

Eventually he softened a bit. Even then I wouldn't back off, but after persistently focusing on the truth of God's Word, he finally broke and started weeping. Turns out his own father deeply wounded him, and his perspective on life, authority, and God had all been affected by his father's abuse. Because he didn't forgive his father, he repeated some of the same offensive behavior toward his own son. Before I left he was softly sobbing like a baby.

Once he saw his error and acknowledged the pastor's and my leadership by apologizing to us, he was able to receive from God in a huge way. The irony of our encounter was he ended up treating me like one of his heroes. This man, who initially acted as if he was going to hurt me, ended up intensely liking me.

Subtle Dishonor

The above example is an extreme case; however, the root attitude is more prevalent with believers than we realize. This man's dishonor was blatant. He wasn't hiding anything, and that actually made it easy to reach him. He was barefaced in his attitude, however, many others are in the same boat, but display their dishonor in a different way. Out of the fear of being labeled as unmannerly or unruly they put on a cooperative face and speak accordingly, but carry dishonor within. It manifests outwardly in more subtle ways.

These I speak of honor leaders with their lips, but their hearts are far from honoring God's appointed servants. It shows outwardly by the way they respond to offerings, change of direction, or various requests made by leadership. The pastor asks the members to attend a special worship night and one-tenth of the congregation shows up. Or he asks the members to come out for a monthly outreach, and maybe one-twentieth shows up.

I go to many churches where thousands attend; anywhere from two to four Sunday services. Usually all but one of those services fills the auditorium. But if the pastor calls for a corporate prayer meeting on Monday night many times you'll only find a couple hundred in attendance. Why? Because of the lack of honor toward the pastor.

You may think, *John, that's a little too extreme.* Let me give another example that could help show it's not. Suppose the pastor announced to all his members on a given Sunday, "We are going to have special Monday night prayer meetings this month. The next four Monday nights we will meet from seven to eight p.m. in the sanctuary." So far, the announcement is not very appealing to 80 percent of the members. Especially since this will interfere with *Monday Night Football.*

Then the pastor makes the statement, "At the conclusion of the final evening of special prayer, I will give a check for five hundred thousand dollars to each person who has attended all four prayer meetings."

What would the attendance be? There wouldn't be any room for all those who show up. People would come early to secure a spot for fear they might not make it into the sanctuary.

How would you respond? Don't kid yourself, because it will withhold what God is possibly trying to show about your own heart.

Ask yourself two questions: First, would you have attended those prayer meetings if your pastor made the announcement without a promised check? Second, would you attend those meetings with the promise of the half million? Think of it, you might be able to pay off your house and car, and have a lot of money left over for other interests.

If your answer was no for the first question and yes for the second, then you've just discovered how little you value your pastor's word. Remember, to honor is to value.

God says, "Obey those who rule over you, and be submissive, for they watch out for your souls" (Heb. 13:17). This is God's instruction to His people; we are to obey our church leaders. So you will do it for the money, but you won't do it just because your pastor, a spokesperson of Jesus Christ, says to do it. So then I must ask, who then is your master? Jesus says the two masters you can obey are God or riches (see Matt. 6:24).

Let's ask some tough questions: Do you show up to service on time? Do you find yourself resisting inside when your pastor asks you to give a special offering? Do you constantly ignore your leader's call for help in the nursery, in ushering, as a parking-lot attendant, in outreach, etc.? Do you find yourself making excuses for why you cannot attend a special Sunday night meeting? Now ask yourself, if the promise were made of five hundred thousand dollars for each of these requests, would you have made a different decision? If so, why? The answer is simple: because the money is more valuable to you than God's representative placed in your life. Recall Jesus' words, "He who receives you receives Me, and he who receives Me receives Him who sent Me" (Matt. 10:40). Again, it could be stated, "He who honors you honors Me, and he who honors Me honors Him who sent Me." When you value your pastor's word, you value God's word, because God has sent him to you.

Now we understand why so many are not thriving in life. We read, "Those who are planted in the house of the LORD shall flourish in the courts of our God" (Ps. 92:13). When we are planted in the local church we will flourish in life, both now and at the judgment seat of Christ. Notice the psalmist doesn't say, "Those who attend the house of the Lord." You can attend a church and not be planted. Being planted means that is where you lay your life down to serve God. It is there you tithe, serve, and obey the leadership. When we are planted we value our local church, just as a tree values the ground from which it receives life.

You may have spurts of prosperity, success, and happiness not being planted in the local church, but you will not experience longevity of these blessings. We shouldn't desire sporadic blessings; rather what endures and brings great pleasure and satisfaction in our latter years, and most of all at the judgment seat of Christ, where all things are revealed.

If you are planted in the church, you will value your church leaders' words. You will not take lightly what they ask of you. You will then fear God, and in fearing God you will honor His appointed leaders. In honoring His appointed leaders you will receive the full reward God has in store for you.

Think Highly of Them

We are instructed, "Dear brothers and sisters, honor those who are your leaders in the Lord's work. They work hard among you and warn you against all that is wrong. Think highly of them and give them your wholehearted love because of their work" (1 Thess. 5:12–13, NLT).

In twenty-five years of ministry, of which seven were in local churches and the rest traveling, I've noticed the believers who are the most fulfilled, peaceful, happy, prosperous, and successful are those who think highly of and give wholehearted love and devotion to their church leaders. God instructs us to do this, so wouldn't it make sense that this testimony is true? The converse is true as well.

Over the years I've come across people on both ends of this spectrum. I've encountered some who see themselves as equally qualified as their pastors. They put up with their leader just because he or she occupies the position. These people think they could do as good a job, or even better, in leading the church or ministry. Often they're biding their time until God "promotes" them into their ministry. They see their pastor as someone who could be easily replaced and treat him no differently than any other person.

Along the same lines, it can be someone who has no aspirations for ministry; they labor in the marketplace and attend church because it is the thing to do. These, unlike the ones described above, see their pastor as filling a role most anyone could fill, especially him- or herself, but they chose a career in the corporate world. They see pastors as inferior in intelligence, which is why they ended up in ministry.

In either case, you'll not find these people succeeding to their full potential in life. Oh, they may do fairly well in business or ministry, but to not near the extent had they planted themselves in the local church and viewed the gift of God, their pastor, as valuable. These most often will experience hardship in their marriage and with their children; they'll suffer medically, financially, and in many other arenas of life.

A Heartbreaking Story

I could give so many examples of those who don't value, and even dishonor, their leaders (and we'll cover the positive end of the spectrum shortly), however, an actual account that so vividly portrays this tragedy occurred with a couple of men I know. I have a friend who pastors a large church. I have ministered in his pulpit regularly for almost ten years, but have known him for over twenty years.

He is respected by the people of his church as well as by numerous national and global leaders.

Years ago he helped a young man discover the direction of God upon his life. This young man, we'll call him Bill, was raised in a denominational group that didn't believe in many of the valuable truths of God's Word. My friend, whom we'll call Randy, led him into the infilling of Holy Spirit and was powerfully used by God to set him on a fruitful course of ministry.

Shortly after, Bill lost his church for embracing the baptism of the Holy Spirit and His gifts. Pastor Randy went with a team of people and packed up all of Bill's household things, which were put on the street by his denomination, and rented an apartment for Bill and his family.

Eventually Bill became a pastor of a thriving church in another city. He started small but through the strong gift of God on his life the church grew rapidly. After a couple years he purchased a movie theater and moved out of the rented storefront space into the reno-vated theater. He invited Pastor Randy to come and help with the building dedication because of the influence Randy had in his life. It was a glorious occasion.

The church continued to thrive, but Bill suffered from a driving addiction that was kept under wraps. It continued to escalate, and the elders of the church eventually became aware of his bondage.

Bill would call Randy periodically to tell him he was going to resign, but not tell him the reason. Pastor Randy encouraged Bill until one day one of the elders called and told Randy Bill's bond-age. Randy immediately got on a plane to come to Bill's side and help. Sadly, the elders, aware of Bill's addiction, still wanted him in the pulpit.

When Randy heard the elders' words he said, "If you even at-tempt to allow Bill to remain in the pulpit I will stay for the ser-vice on Sunday and publicly expose the situation. You do not care for his family; you only care for yourselves and the church. But if you accept his resignation, I will be available to help the church transition."

That same day Pastor Randy rescued Bill and his family, paid for them to move near his church, and found Bill a good-paying job. Over time Bill recovered under Randy's ministry.

Randy later brought Bill onto his staff as one of his associate pastors to help get him back on track with the call of God on his life. In the meantime Christian publications wrote stories of Bill's deliverance, and his notoriety grew as a result of his testimony. After a while Bill was given an offer to come to another ministry and teach along with the encouragement to set up his own traveling ministry. Pastor Randy felt Bill was not yet ready to make this move and advised otherwise. Bill felt his pastor was controlling and hindering his destiny; so he ignored Randy's counsel and moved on.

Time passed and eventually Bill and I had an opportunity for dinner with another couple of leaders. Bill spent much of our time together complaining about Pastor Randy. He was critical of how Randy ran the church, the treatment he received while on staff, and his former pastor's lack of agreeing with his departure. I recall vividly the alarm I felt in my heart. I knew he was offended, which led to a steep decline in the way he viewed the man who did so much for his life.

I defended Randy at that dinner but could see I was getting nowhere. I knew it was wrong to discuss these things without Randy being there to give his side of the story. So I ended our discussion by telling Bill that Randy was a father in the faith to him, and even if Randy was wrong (which I was careful to not say he was), Bill was wrong to speak critically of him and dishonor him. I shared with him other biblical examples I've shared earlier in this book, but Bill was relentless in his disapproval of Pastor Randy.

Several months later I received a call from Pastor Randy. I can still hear the sadness in his voice. It was as if someone died. Bill published a book, and one of the chapters dealt with how to respond to controlling churches and leaders. Randy said, "John, I want to read to you four pages of Bill's new book." He proceeded to read Bill's slanderous report of Randy, his staff, and his church. Though no names were mentioned, it was obvious who he was writing about; after all this was the only church at which he'd held the position of associate pastor. From what was stated in Bill's book you would have thought Pastor Randy was a monstrous control freak. (The interesting fact is, in the ten years I've traveled to Randy's church, there has been very little turnover with his large staff. They are very devoted and love him dearly.)

After finishing the four pages, Randy said, "John, I can handle this on a personal level; however, my pain comes from the members of our church [which numbered in the thousands] who could read this, and you know many of them will read it since he was a pastor here. This could easily poison them, which will hinder their ability to receive from God any longer in our church."

I was heartbroken. I couldn't believe what my ears heard. Randy rescued Bill out of a situation few would touch. He took Bill in, cared for him, and restored him. How could Bill have done this? I knew he sowed seeds of dishonor, and the harvest would not be pretty. In fact it would be devastating, unless he repented.

A few years later Bill took another pastorate position. He again caused the church to grow through the gift of God on his life. (The gift of God will operate to a measure of success, even if we are out of line with God's heart.) However, the harvest was due to come in. He again fell into his old bondage. This time it was even worse, as it directly devastated another family. The consequences rippled through the church and community. The church was left in a crippled state; many were offended and disillusioned. Today, Bill is no longer in ministry.

Had Bill honored his spiritual father I believe he would have been sent out into his own ministry at the proper time; would not have fallen a second time; and to this day would be a shining witness of how God can deliver and restore us from sin. However, now due to dishonoring his spiritual father, we have a tragedy that has wounded too many. It could have been avoided. By telling this story, I'm hopeful this tragedy can be avoided in the lives of others.

Bill has an amazing gift on his life to teach the Word of God. In fact, I used to marvel at the revelations given to him. I've heard others who knew him and sat under his ministry comment about the power of his teachings. How tragic. If Bill would have honored his spiritual father, it would have gone well with him and those he influenced.

The apostle Paul states, "For though you might have ten thousand instructors in Christ, yet you do not have many fathers" (1 Cor. 4:15). We must remember God says we come under a curse when we dishonor our father. Not only does this apply to our natural fathers, but spiritual fathers as well. I personally believe a lot of tragic mishaps could have been avoided if those involved would have developed true honor within their hearts and guarded themselves from offense, especially in regard to their spiritual fathers and mothers.

Two or Three Witnesses

The man who first put me in ministry lost his entire church of eight thousand members; the church no longer exists today, due to the pastor leaving his wife for a younger woman. He told the congregation he was leaving his wife and if they didn't like it they could leave and go to another church. It was a devastating blow. Tragically, many men followed his course of action and divorced their own wives in the church.

Many who served by my side when I worked for this church became very critical of this man. I, too, started down the same path. I was frustrated and angry with him. The honor I held in my heart for him as my spiritual father was rapidly decaying. I left the church five years earlier. He released Lisa and me with blessing for a new position of ministry in another state, but even though we were no longer at the church I was growing more frustrated and angry with him.

Then over a two-week period I had four dreams of my former pastor. I rarely remember my dreams. So for me to have four dreams in two weeks that I remembered was completely out of the ordinary. I'm almost embarrassed to write this, but it wasn't until after the fourth dream that I finally realized God was trying to say something to me. I went to prayer and asked, "Father, what are You showing me through these dreams?"

Immediately I heard a stern voice say, "He's My servant, stop judging My servant!"

It was not my place to criticize or pass judgment on my former pastor, who was a father to me. Once I realized this I repented and wrote him a letter of apology.

A couple months after divorcing his wife he married a young blonde woman and shortly afterward the church dwindled to four hundred members. He tried to save the church, but it was only a matter of time before the doors were permanently closed. Should you leave a church if a pastor is in open sin and will not repent of it? The answer is absolutely yes. Paul writes,

> I wrote you in my [previous] letter not to associate [closely and habitually] with unchaste (impure) people—Not [meaning of course that you must] altogether shun the immoral people of this world, or the greedy graspers and cheats and thieves or idolaters, since otherwise you would need to get out of the world and human society altogether! But now I write to you not to associate with anyone who bears the

name of [Christian] brother if he is known to be guilty of immorality or greed, or is an idolater [whose soul is devoted to any object that usurps the place of God], or is a person with a foul tongue [railing, abusing, reviling, slandering], or is a drunkard or a swindler *or* a robber. [No] you must not so much as eat with such a person.

—1 Cor. 5:9–11 (AMP)

Paul clearly states we are not to closely associate with a "Christian" who lives in immorality. For this leader to divorce his wife for the reason of not getting along—all the while having a younger woman in the wings waiting to marry—this is immorality. According to Jesus, it's really quite clear, for He states, "I say to you, whoever divorces his wife, except for sexual immorality, and marries another, commits adultery" (Matt. 19:9).

So if we are not to eat with a "Christian" who is living in willful sin, then we are certainly not to partake of their spirit; we are not to sit under a man's ministry who's in this state. If he repents, then we can receive from him once again.

You may now ask, "But John, isn't that judging him?" To answer, it would actually be judging his fruit. We are to judge fruit—men's actions—but not their heart motives. Paul says, "It isn't my responsibility to judge outsiders, but it certainly is your job to judge those inside the church who are sinning in these ways" (1 Cor. 5:12, NLT).

Without going into detail, I was judging my pastor's heart motive, and for this reason God had to warn me through dreams. Only God can judge a man's heart motives. Paul says,

"Therefore judge nothing before the time, until the Lord comes, who will both bring to light the hidden things of darkness and reveal the counsels (*motives*) of the hearts."

—1 Cor. 4:5 (words in parentheses mine)

For this reason I stay hopeful for my former pastor's life.

To help clarify this, just yesterday I was talking with a person in ministry who was disturbed by a message another minister brought forth in a conference. This friend was processing the sermon on the phone with me and was bringing up scripture to clearly show the error in this message. I agreed with everything this person was saying in regard to the message (other ministers expressed the same concerns). However, the person on the phone went on to say, "I think this minister came up with this teaching in order to have a unique message that will open doors to many larger churches and conferences."

I immediately stopped this friend on the phone and said, "You are now judging his motives, and that is wrong."

I told my friend it was fine to judge the fruit—what is said or done, in this case the actual message—but not the motive. Only God can do that. This is what I was doing with my pastor and why God gave me a stern warning.

Those four hundred who stayed under my former pastor's leadership after he married the young woman entered into a very perverted ministry situation. Their loyalty was not scriptural. They stayed in an atmosphere of a wrong spirit, not the Holy Spirit.

To this day I still honor my former pastor, even though he has not publicly repented (he is married to a third wife now). If he had a church I wouldn't sit under his ministry, but he will hold a place of honor in my heart for the rest of my life. Recall even after God judged Saul, David still honored him by singing a love song to him, and taught the men of Judah to do the same. If my former pastor called me today for help, I would assist as much as I could and as fast as possible. He taught me so many wonderful truths of the Word of God, the benefit of which I'm still enjoying to this day; he believed in me and gave me opportunity when no one else did. When I was green and raw and made many mistakes, he forgave and encouraged me. I will always honor him. Even in writing this, which I do only to help others, I grieve in my heart for the pain he and others effected by his choices lived through. My hope is he will repent and rebound to the great leader he once was. Scripture states God's hopes are fadeless and do not weaken (see 1 Cor. 13:7).

On the flip side, many today will leave churches because they hear rumors of their pastor committing sin. No, a thousand times no! We should not listen to rumors. We are told, "Do not receive an accusation against an elder except from two or three witnesses" (1 Tim. 5:19).

A witness is one who has irrefutable evidence that could stand up in a court of law. Not two people, who are conspiring together, or a few people who are spreading the same rumor. No, two or three people who have separate evidence. Why does Paul write this? To protect us.

Think of it, if we believe a rumor of a leader it opens the door to suspicion or inaccurate belief. Dishonor easily enters our hearts. If we dishonor the leader we can no longer receive the reward God has to give us through that leader. This is why so many Westerners have difficulty receiving from God. In our generation there's been a great amount of scandal in ministry, which has fostered suspicion in the hearts of multitudes. Many are jaded, and even cynical, in the church today; an attitude that doesn't at all cultivate honor. This has been the enemy's plot to hold us back and keep us from the receiving channels of heaven, God's leaders.

Hannah was able to receive from Eli even though eventually the gluttonous and greedy life he lived would be exposed, and judgment would result. She kept her heart free from a cynical attitude, even when she felt the brunt of Eli's deteriorated character in calling her a "drunk." She acted, rather than reacted. Many today react to the heartbreaks of ministry failure, to which some of our Western church leaders have succumbed.

In years of ministry I've heard numerous negative reports of leaders, but I have a personal conviction rooted in the above scripture from 1 Timothy that directs my life. I automatically disregard a negative report if it only comes from one person, or if there is no concrete evidence from at least two people. I must have separate evidence from at least two people to believe the report. If I put any weight in these reports it will block my ability to receive from heaven. All leaders carry a reward from heaven. I personally don't want to miss a thing God has for me, and I believe you feel the same way.

The Other End of the Spectrum

In looking at the other end of the spectrum, I've come to know, and grown to love, many in the church who have honored and given their wholehearted love and devotion to leaders. Some are on staffs of churches, some are associates to the leaders, and many others are members of churches or partners with these ministers.

It has been a delight to watch God promote these people over the years. Sometimes it doesn't look as though they are moving up the scale of responsibility or being promoted rapidly, but after watching many of them over the course of ten, twenty, or even twenty-five years, I've seen steady, but sure, increase in their lives in every good way.

I recall many were very upset with my original pastor whom I discussed earlier; they developed attitudes that didn't cultivate honor. They became critical, and many suffered tragic results. Some divorced, some suffered terrible things with their children, some went through financial ruin, others took over or started churches and after years of labor couldn't grow their churches past one or two hundred. In an extreme case I recall one woman who worked with me who went on TV and spoke against my pastor (the one who lost the entire church). She was in perfect health, but two months later she died suddenly of a massive brain aneurism. Do I think that was coincidence? No, Paul states many believers do not discern the Lord's body and because of this many are "weak and sick among you, and many sleep (die prematurely)" (1 Cor. 11:30, words in parentheses mine). Paul wrote this in the context of communion. However, the truth applies to other areas of Christian living as well. There is much more to discerning the Lord's body than drinking grape juice and eating a cracker.

On the other hand, I saw numerous men and women, who suffered at the hand of my former pastor, keep a heart of love and honor toward him, no different than David, and they are all very successful today! I've seen them prosper in ministry, in business, in life. Their marriages have stayed strong; their children have stayed in love with God and have prospered. They are living a rich and full life because they have walked in honor and integrity. They've guarded their hearts and put a watch over their mouths. They've pleased the heart of God.

Why wouldn't anyone want the good life God desires for us? Is it really worth becoming critical, cynical, or jaded? What fruit does it produce? In seeing the long-term results, I don't want anything to do with this type of attitude, no matter how I've been treated by a leader. It's just not worth it. But most important of all reasons is this: those in the Bible who honored their leaders were those who stayed close to the heart of God. That to me is the greatest of all rewards, to know His heart and have deep fellowship with Him. There's nothing greater in life.

CHAPTER 11

Double Honor

∞

Let the elders who rule well be counted worthy of double honor, especially those who labor in the word and doctrine. For the Scripture says, "You shall not muzzle an ox while it treads out the grain," and, "The laborer is worthy of his wages."

—1 TIMOTHY 5:17–18

This is the only place in all of Scripture you will find "double honor" in regard to authority. We're to give ministers of the gospel twice as much honor as we would to other leaders.

Practically speaking, how is this done? Our behavior and speech toward Christian leaders should be with the utmost respect. We should address them formally, such as "Pastor," "Sir," "Mr.," or "Mrs.," etc., unless they instruct us otherwise. We should keep eye contact with them at all times during conversation, and not leave until dismissed, or we know they are finished speaking with us.

When a leader teaches the Word we should listen attentively. To allow our mind to wander is to dishonor. Remember, honor is shown not just in action and word, but also in thought. For this reason Paul exhorts us, "Give attention to reading, to exhortation, to doctrine" (1 Tim. 4:13).

To converse with someone sitting by us while in a service is to dishonor the one speaking, not to mention the Holy Spirit Himself. All personal interaction should be held off until after the meeting. Nor should we text-message our friends, use our cell phones, or exit the service until formally dismissed. We shouldn't come to the meeting or service late. How would our employers respond to our coming in fifteen minutes late to work every morning? We wouldn't think of doing this. Why should we do the same in regard to scheduled service times our leaders have set?

We should look for ways to serve our leaders without being asked. Plan ahead for them, and be on the alert for unforeseen obstacles. We should always seek to do things better and with a higher standard. We should strive for excellence in all we do in representing them.

If you are asked to run an errand for your leader, be prompt and do it with excellence. Don't go with inappropriate attire or a dirty vehicle. You should represent your leader well. I've been picked up at the airport before in cars that were cluttered with trash and junk. I thought to myself, *How would the leader of this ministry feel if he knew his employee was picking up his guest in this manner? He's dishonored not only me but the pastor who asked him to be my host.*

Lisa and I have a great staff of approximately fifty people. I'm amazed at how they treat us. When arriving at my office there is always a fresh glass of purified water sitting on my desk. Many times when I'm not looking they secure my car keys, run it to the gas station, and fuel it, even if the car still has a good amount of gas in it. They make sure the car is clean at all times. I don't have a formal parking spot in our office building, but the staff always leaves the spot closest to the front door open for Lisa or me.

They stand when I come into their office or walk into a conference room, and they address me as "sir." They always make sure they've researched a matter thoroughly before bringing it to me.

They anticipate my questions and have answers prepared before I ask. Any request I make always gets done promptly, and if one avenue to complete the job meets a roadblock, they will keep pounding away until the job gets done. Only if the task is impossible is it not accomplished. But before this news is brought to me they will have gone down every possible road imaginable, and will have alternatives to the original request.

The honor they show us is strong and purposeful. To keep it from getting out of place in my mind, I first and foremost remember that in honoring me, they are honoring Jesus. Second, I'm fully aware of the reward they'll receive. Thirdly, I keep in mind why they serve us; they don't want our energies being given to things that will distract us from our assignment. The more Lisa and I can focus on what God has called us to do, the more people are served. It's all about serving in the Kingdom, and when we honor one another (I will get to how we honor our staff in upcoming chapters) each of us is more effective in pleasing God.

Lisa and I do not seek honor. For a leader to seek or demand honor is out of step with the heart of God. Jesus said, "I crave no human honor" (John 5:41, AMP). He sought only the honor that came from His Father. He rebuked the leaders of His day by saying, "No wonder you can't believe! For you gladly honor each other, but you don't care about the honor that comes from God alone" (John 5:44, NLT). These leaders sought the praise and honor of men in order to feed their ego, pride, and controlling personalities. Jesus received honor from men and women for their sake, and most of all for His Father's sake.

We, too, as believers must fully realize the honor given to us is to be passed in our hearts to Jesus and the Father; and we should rejoice for the sake of those who give it. We are fully aware the Father will in turn honor those who honor us; they will receive a reward. I can't emphasize this point enough: no matter who you are, if you look to be honored for any other reason you are heading down a path that does not lead to life and godliness.

Double Finances

There are vast scenarios I could write about in giving "double honor" to ministers of the gospel. However, I've not yet touched the specifics of what the Holy Spirit is saying through the apostle Paul in 1 Timothy 5:17–18. If we continue to read we discover he is particularly referring to finances. Paul completes his statement with, "The laborer is worthy of his wages." The New Living Translation reads, "Elders who do their work well should be paid well." The Contemporary English Version states, "Church leaders who do their job well deserve to be paid twice as much, especially if they work hard at preaching and teaching." The Today's English Version reads, "The elders who do good work as leaders should be considered worthy of receiving double pay." And finally the Amplified Bible states elders who perform their duties well are to be considered doubly worthy, "of adequate financial support."

Again, this spiritual principle is found in the words of Jesus to His disciples: "Most assuredly, I say to you, he who *honors* whomever I send *honors* Me; and he who *honors* Me *honors* Him who sent Me" (John 13:20, the word *receives* has been changed to *honors*). Notice the words "*whomever I send.*" You can see how Jesus personalizes this. We also see this in the way Paul describes how the fivefold leadership has been commissioned and sent:

> And His [*Jesus Christ's*] gifts were [varied; He himself appointed and gave men to us] some to be apostles (special messengers), some prophets (inspired preachers and expounders), some evangelists (preachers of the Gospel, traveling missionaries), some pastors (shepherds of His flock) and teachers.
>
> —Ephesians 4:11 (AMP)

Notice the words "He himself appointed." Jesus personally gives the fivefold minister. These are the elders within the body of Christ "who labor in the word and doctrine" (1 Tim. 5:17). God specifically states they are to be honored by being paid "twice as much" (CEV).

In over twenty years of travels I've never seen an exception to this command. I've gone to churches where the pastor and associate pastors are not paid well. They drive older-model cars, live in rented or undesirable homes; all the while many of the members of the church live in nicer homes and drive nicer cars, their children attend better schools, etc. However, the ironic fact is this: in investigating the financial condition of the members, you find most are struggling. The businessmen and women are constantly experiencing setbacks and even long-term losses. As a result many are in debt over their heads. Many families frequently are faced with problems that eat up their reserves. No one seems to have the extra cash to help others in need. Could this be a result of the believers ignoring God's command to pay their leaders well?

More light is shed by the converse of what I've just stated. I've also gone to many churches where the pastor and associates are paid very well. They all drive nice cars and live in nice homes, their children do not lack, they are able to take nice vacations as families, and the list continues. Many times the people of the church do special things for these ministers: buy them gifts, treat them to a nice dinner, and other gestures of kindness. In observing the families in these churches, on the whole, if they've been planted in the church for any length of time, they are prospering and living successful lives. The businessmen and women are constantly coming upon successful ventures and greatly prospering. They are always quick to help widows, single mothers, or families in need because they have the extra resources to do so. On the whole, these churches are able to do far more in mission giving than the ones described earlier. I've never once seen an exception. This shouldn't surprise us; it all falls in line with the honor principle.

So think of it. The first set of churches I mentioned boast of not wasting their finances in adequately paying their pastor and associates. The mind-set is they can now do more for the Kingdom: give to missions, help the poor, and so forth. However, because of shunning God's command to pay their elders well, they aren't able to reach out to the needy near as much as other churches, because their businesspeople struggle and consequently don't take in as much. Why can't we just realize the wisdom of God is always the path of true success? When we refrain from acting on what God says in His Word because we believe we can do more to help His cause, in reality it's pride—false humility. We indirectly communicate we know more than God, because God loves the poor, but at the same time tells us to pay those who labor in His Word doubly.

I realize this truth has been abused, especially by a small percentage of ministers in America. I grieve when leaders constantly talk about money and material things. They live an opulent lifestyle and are more focused on temporal things and a pleasure-filled lifestyle than reaching lost and hurting souls. They have a truth, but have lost the heartbeat of ministry, and have veered to the path of hirelings. Now their preaching is skewed, and they've lost their effectiveness. Hear what God says to leaders such as these:

> For the leaders of my people—the LORD's watchmen, his shepherds—are blind to every danger. They are like silent watchdogs that give no warning when danger comes. They love to lie around, sleeping and dreaming. And they are as greedy as dogs, never satisfied. They are stupid shepherds, all following their own path, all of them intent on personal gain.
>
> —Isaiah 56:10–11 (NLT)

Notice the final words "all of them intent on personal gain." The CEV states, "You are shepherds who mistreat your own sheep for selfish gain." There are some leaders (glad to say it is very few) who have used women of the church, money, and other assets designated for the ministry for their own personal pleasure. They've taken this truth of honor to a perverted place. They've come to a dark mind-set—the whole intent has been turned around; the ministry is now given to serve them. They've departed from the true focus of ministry—to adequately serve God's people and reach out to the lost. If they do not change, their end will be very dark.

So yes, in the ministry down through the years and in the Bible there has been abuse to the honor principle; but we must ask, should this abuse cause us to veer away from the scriptural command of giving double financial honor to God's servants? Two wrongs have never made a right in God's eyes.

An Amazing Turnaround

The most vivid example I've witnessed of the consequences of withholding financial honor from a church leader happened early in our traveling years. I recall my wife and I drove to minister in a church of approximately 120 people. This church had been in existence for years and its membership fluctuated from 35 to 120 members. It couldn't break into new levels of effectiveness in reaching the community, and the surrounding area had over 250,000 residents.

We were scheduled to conduct a four-day meeting. The pastor asked if we could stay in his house, as it would be a strain on the church to put us up in a hotel. We agreed, as they were also friends of ours long before we started traveling.

We arrived on Saturday night, and I noticed the couple didn't live in a house but a rented duplex. Their car was old, and they didn't have a lot, but what they had they made completely available to us. The wife's hospitality was extraordinary, and they were a very kind and compassionate couple. I was surprised the wife was still working a job requiring frequent travel. She was out of town roughly fifteen to eighteen days a month.

The meetings went fairly well, however, there was a certain strain in the atmosphere. We just couldn't get a breakthrough in God's presence, power, and anointing. There seemed to be a blockage to receiving from heaven. The people of the church were cordial, and many seemed to love God deeply. I was puzzled.

I spent considerable time in prayer on the third day of the meetings. My spirit was agitated and I couldn't put my finger on the problem or shake it off. While in prayer I kept thinking how this pastor and his wife were not being cared for financially. Finally I heard God say, "You must deal with this issue in tonight's service."

I asked how, and God revealed the way to break this barrier was to teach the people the importance of financially blessing their pastor. I felt strongly to take an offering for them personally. I still didn't know precisely how I would accomplish this.

That afternoon the pastor said to me, "John, I'm not going to take the offering for your ministry tonight. I would like you to do it."

I smiled, knowing I now had the open door. Instead of taking the offering for our ministry I would take it for the pastor and his wife. When the pastor introduced me that night, as I stepped onto the platform he whispered to me, "Remember John, you have total liberty in the offering."

I just smiled. I knew he'd be totally surprised by my course of action. I stood behind the pulpit and asked the church to open their Bibles to 1 Timothy 5:17. I proceeded to teach the next forty-five minutes the importance of financially taking care of their pastor.

If I can write this without sounding pompous, I rebuked this congregation sternly. At one point I said, "Why is your pastor's wife working an outside job and having to travel half the month? This couple should be financially sound enough for her to stay home by his side."

The pastor's face kept getting redder and redder; he was nervous with the confrontation. He was scared the people were going to think he put me up to it, and feared an exodus of several families. (I want to clarify a point. I will not go into a church and bring a thought that is not a foundational doctrine if I know the leader disagrees with what I'm saying. In this case, I was not aware. I simply noticed concern develop on his face as the message progressed.)

I can happily say the church received what God placed in my heart that evening. At the conclusion of the message I made this statement: "I was asked to take an offering for our ministry tonight. However, we will not do this. Tonight's offering will go to the pastor and his wife personally; and by the way, you will not get a tax deduction for this gift. I want you to show your appreciation for the gift of God—your pastor."

We took the offering and the service was closed. Afterward I talked with several people, and the pastor slipped away to the church offices. Once I discovered he left the sanctuary, I also headed that way. When I found him I couldn't help noticing his face was no longer red; it now was white. I already knew the news would be good. I grinned and asked, "How much was the offering?"

He gave the figure. I about fainted. It was more than three times the largest Sunday morning offering ever taken. I knew it would be good, but what they reported to me was way beyond what I could have imagined a church of this size could do.

The next Monday I got a call from the pastor. With an excited voice he said, "John, I'm sending you a tape of Sunday's service."

I was caught off guard by his offer and remarked, "Okay, I'll listen to what you preached yesterday."

He quickly responded, "John, I didn't preach. For two solid hours the members of my congregation spontaneously came running up to the platform and testified of the amazing financial miracles that happened this week in their homes and businesses. I was in awe, but wasn't surprised. I knew God would do an amazing work, but I didn't realize it would be so quick."

Three years later I returned to the church. They no longer met in a storefront; they renovated and moved into a high school. That's not all. The church didn't rent the high school; they bought it! Their attendance grew five times in size. The pastor's wife was able to leave her job because he was honored financially, and the families and businesspeople of the church prospered as a result.

"Don't Say I Like Something"

It never fails. If we will honor our spiritual leaders financially, we will prosper in our own lives. I look at Dr. David Cho, pastor of the world's largest church in Seoul, South Korea. He started the church in a dump years ago, and at the time of this writing I've been told by two of his board members he now has over fifty thousand millionaires in his congregation.

I've hosted him on a few occasions, played golf with him, and eaten in restaurants with him and his traveling companions. He usually comes with several businessmen and associates. These men make sure he is well cared for; they will buy him anything he needs, and I've taken particular note of how they will not sit down for a meal until he is first seated. They honor him greatly. Could the reason the church, which was started in a very poor section of the city, has so many wealthy members be the honor they show their pastor?

I have a close friend named Al Brice. He pastors here in the United States and is on the leadership board of our ministry. Al played in the United States Amateur golf tournament in 1980; he is an excellent golfer. Dr. Cho enjoys playing golf along with many of his associates and friends, so he took a particular liking to Al.

On a certain occasion Dr. Cho and his associates were here in the States and were scheduled to play golf with Al. One of the men traveling with Dr. Cho got out of their rental car and pulled out his golf clubs. He had just bought a brand-new designer golf bag while on New York's Fifth Avenue that cost thousands of dollars. Al, to be gracious, commented on how beautiful it was. Suddenly, to Al's surprise, this man started pulling his clubs out of his brand-new bag. Once emptied, he then grabbed Al's clubs out of his bag and started putting them in his designer bag. Al urgently spoke, "No, stop, what are doing?"

The Korean man said, "I'm honoring you, I want to give this bag to you." My friend tried to stop him, but he would not be talked out of it.

A few months later Al was over in Korea and again getting ready to play golf with Dr. Cho and his associates. He saw a handsome pair of golf shoes in the pro shop and commented, "Wow, those are great-looking shoes."

One of Dr. Cho's men immediately pulled the shoes off the shelf and started for the cash register. Al said, "No, no, I don't need any shoes. I was only commenting on how nice they were."

The man said, "No sir, I honor you, I want you to have them."

When Al shared this with me, he laughed in an affectionate way and said, "I've learned to not say I like something around Dr. Cho's men, because they will buy it for me." These believers walk in a high degree of honor and are blessed because of it.

A Blessed Life

I have another friend, Jack, who has gone to be with the Lord. He lived a very successful and powerful life. Hundreds of thousands were greatly affected by his ministry.

When Jack was young and just starting in the ministry, his pastor also had a very well-respected church in the United States. After serving his pastor for years, Jack was launched into another part of the country to start a church.

The church reached the five-thousand mark within a few years.

I preached frequently for him, and we loved spending time together. I recall vividly one day he was commenting to me of how much he loved, valued, and respected his former pastor. He referred to him as his spiritual father. Jack then said, "John, every time I see my pastor I make it a point to give him a thousand-dollar check." I was amazed at the level of honor.

His comment caused me to think of how great a reward he was living in. His church members loved him deeply. In fact, his funeral lasted over four hours and the building was packed to capacity. Over five thousand attended—not only church members, but also many laborers in his city who didn't attend his church. So many in the community respected him.

Jack's church honored him. They desired to pay him handsomely, but because of smart investing he didn't have to receive a salary from the church. He chose to donate it back to the ministry. I have not seen many men who have walked in the blessing of God as this man did. His wife and daughters loved him passionately. He lived in a beautiful home and had many friends. Jack honored his spiritual father financially; it positioned him for a very handsome reward in many other areas of life.

In Our Meetings

In traveling and ministering in churches around the world, I've observed the results of ministry are vastly different in those that take care of our team with exceptional hospitality, and those who treat us as common travelers.

I've gone to places where I wondered why they asked me to come. They put us in run-down hotels or outside-entrance hotels; they have no bottled water or snacks in the room, and no room service available. I'm greeted in the pastor's office not with warmth and gratefulness for coming, but with more of an attitude of: *I'm expecting this out of you.* I've been treated by a few with the attitude of, "What we are doing here is important and you're privileged to speak here."

When I'm introduced the people sit and stare at me with a disinterested look. You can almost hear their thoughts: *We've heard them all, what do you have that is any different?* As I speak I feel as if I'm on trial.

I come out of these meetings feeling worn out. I've spiritually plowed through the resistance the entire time, rather than being drawn from hungry hearts. Then the pastor will hand me an offering check so small that if his church received this amount every week they could not survive. I'm happy to report, this doesn't happen frequently.

I recall one specific incident: I was asked to speak at a conference with another minister for an entire week. The pastor shared that they had taken in over two hundred and fifty thousand dollars for the meetings. I was very happy for them. However, when I left they handed me a six-hundred-dollar check for our ministry. Barely a tip, and not a good one either; just 10 percent would have been twenty-five thousand. So it was a little more than two-tenths of a percent (that's 0.2 percent).

I've learned it doesn't affect our ministry, because God always gets us what we need through some other avenue. Every time in the past when churches have tipped us in this manner (I guess I really can't describe that as a tip, because it is far below tipping standards) we get a huge gift in the mail the same week from an individual or we'll go to the next church and they'll give us an enormous offering. I love it, because it is as if God is saying to us, "I know."

I've seen the faithfulness of God to supply for us, and I've never lost any sleep over it. My grief is for those who gave the crumbs; they've missed out on an opportunity to receive a great reward by honoring the one Jesus sent them.

On the flip side I've gone to meetings where from the moment I was picked up at the airport until the time I was dropped off again, I was met with excitement and treated with extreme kindness and genuine hospitality.

I arrive in my hotel room and am welcomed with a large basket of fruit, drinks, and snacks that I could feed on for a week. The church checked with our office for what types of foods I like to snack on. I've even arrived to find presents awaiting me in my hotel room, such as a candle, nice pen, shirt, or cologne. They put me in the nicest hotels in the area and make sure I have room service and other amenities that make living on the road more like home. Not only do they do this for me, but for my traveling assistants as well.

When I step in the pulpits I'm greeted with the people standing and giving a loud applause. They are thankful to God for sending them one of His messengers, and are excitedly anticipating hearing the Word of God. They listen to the Word attentively; no one moves or talks during the service, because they don't want to miss one point. They welcome the presence of God during ministry time, and finally rush our resource tables to glean more from the books and curriculums.

These churches will talk with our office or me months and even years later and make comments like, "We turned the corner when you came," or "Our staff and church has never been the same. It was as if we went up to another level." I sometimes laugh inside, because maybe just the week prior I went to a church that treated us as common travelers. I ministered on the same subject and came with the same purpose, but the results were very small, and no comments were made after I left. It again shows it has nothing to do with me, but how I'm received.

Jesus says, "He who receives you receives Me, and he who receives Me receives Him who sent Me." How would you want Jesus cared for if He was the pastor of your church, or if He visited your church to minister on a certain weekend? The fact is, the way we treat those He sends us is exactly how we treat Him, and it is exactly how we treat the Father.

Honor the Lord

Let's look again at the honor principle. God says, "Those who honor Me I will honor, and those who despise Me shall be lightly esteemed" (1 Sam. 2:30).

This scripture needs to be etched in our souls. Those who honor God, He honors in return. Say it aloud: "If I honor God, He will honor me." Recite it over and over, ponder it, and let it sink deep within your heart. To honor God is to attract His honor toward you. It's an amazing reality! Let's take this truth further; we read,

> "Honor the LORD with your possessions, and with the first-fruits of all your increase."
>
> —Prov. 3:9

We are told to honor God with our possessions. The Amplified Bible reads, "Honor the Lord with your capital and sufficiency [from righteous labors] and with the firstfruits of all your income." The CEV reads, "Honor the LORD by giving him your money." One way we honor God is by giving Him our money. My question is, how can we give Him money? He doesn't use our currency. The answer is simple—in giving it to the one He sends you.

If you study tithes and offerings carefully throughout the Bible you'll find they are given for three main purposes. The first is to provide for the appointed servants who minister to us, and as we saw clearly earlier in this chapter, they are worthy of "double pay." Secondly, to provide for the minister's needs to do the work of the ministry; and third, so that they can help the poor, the widows, the orphans and the outsiders.

I'd like to give you just one of the many scriptures relating to each purpose. The first is seen in Paul's words to the Corinthians: "If we have sown spiritual things for you, is it a great thing if we reap your material things? ... Even so the Lord has commanded that those who preach the gospel should live from the gospel" (1 Cor. 9:11, 14).

The NLT reads as follows: "The Lord gave orders that those who preach the Good News should be supported by those who benefit from it." This principle is also seen in the Old Testament. The priests' and Levites' inheritances were to come from the tithes of the people. They were not given land to work as the other tribes.

The second point is seen in Paul's words to the Philippian church:

> And you Philippians yourselves well know that in the early days of the Gospel ministry, when I left Macedonia, no church (assembly) entered into partnership with me *and* opened up [a debit and credit] account in giving and receiving except you only. For even in Thessalonica you sent [me contributions] for my needs, not only once but a second time. . . . But I have [your full payment] and more; I have everything I need and am amply supplied, now that I have received from Epaphroditus the gifts you sent me. [They are the] fragrant odor of an offering *and* sacrifice which God welcomes *and* in which He delights.
>
> —Philippians 4:15–16, 18 (AMP)

You can see their financial gifts enabled Paul to accomplish the work to which he was called. Simply put, it takes money to conduct a public ministry. In his own words, Paul was "amply supplied." Through giving they entered into a partnership with him in reaching others.

As for the third point, in the Old Testament God instructed that the tithe was to be given to the Levite (minister), stranger, fatherless, and widow (see Deut. 26:12). In the New Testament the leaders all agreed: "They desired only that we should remember the poor, the very thing which I also was eager to do" (Gal. 2:10).

The poor would include the stranger, orphan, and widow. By giving to ministers, we can help those in need we may never meet.

As already stated, we honor God with our finances by giving to those He's selected for ministry. So we must ask, how many today dishonor God by withholding more than they should from the work of the ministry? Many don't tithe, and many don't give offerings to the laborers who have sown spiritual truths into their lives. They complain of hearing ministers ask for money, and make statements such as, "Why can't they just preach to me without talking about offerings? Things have not gone well for me lately." Could this be why they are struggling? They've not put God's work first? So in essence they honor themselves more than they honor God.

This is what the LORD Almighty says: Consider how things are going for you! You have planted much but harvested little. You have food to eat, but not enough to fill you up. You have wine to drink, but not enough to satisfy your thirst. You have clothing to wear, but not enough to keep you warm. Your wages disappear as though you were putting them in pockets filled with holes! This is what the LORD Almighty says: Consider how things are going for you! Now go up into the hills, bring down timber, and rebuild my house. Then I will take pleasure in it and be honored, says the LORD. You hoped for rich harvests, but they were poor. And when you brought your harvest home, I blew it away. Why? Because my house lies in ruins, says the LORD Almighty, while you are all busy building your own fine houses.

—Haggai 1:5–9 (NLT)

How clear can it be? Suppose some of the people we admire in Scripture would have had the attitude many have today in regard to ministers talking about money in hard times. There were many widows who died in the days of Elijah during the great famine. However, one lived because of the honor principle. She and her son had only enough flour and oil to make a final meal; then they would both die. However, the prophet told her to make him a cake first. Wow, would he have gotten persecuted today, both in churches and by the media. Many would criticize, "How could you take anything from a poor woman who is about to suffer starvation? You should give to her first." However, the Word of the Lord instructed the prophet to tell her to put God first by feeding His servant; if she would honor him in this way, God would honor her. She did, and God did what He promised; her flour and oil never ran out the entire duration of the drought (see 1 Kings 17).

When we withhold the tithe or offerings from those God sends us, we harm only ourselves because we dishonor the Lord. God Himself speaks through the prophet:

"Will a man rob God? Yet you have robbed Me! But you say, 'In what way have we robbed You?' In tithes and offerings."

—Mal. 3:8

If I had to make a choice, I would rather rob a bank than God Himself. Why? Because I fear God more than man. I'm so glad I don't have to choose; I would never want to rob either. However, God says, "You have robbed Me!" Notice He didn't say, "You've robbed My ministers!" No, we rob God by not tithing and giving offerings to His servants, because to withhold from the servants He sends us is to dishonor Him. Hear what He continues to say: " 'Bring all the tithes into the storehouse, that there may be food in My house, and try Me now in this,' says the LORD of hosts, 'If I will not open for you the windows of heaven and pour out for you such blessing that there will not be room enough to receive it' " (v. 10).

Notice God Himself states that the blessing of tithing would be so great there will "not be room enough to receive it." So in essence, the blessing will be an *uncontainable* commodity. For years I've heard ministers say that God will bless our finances and possessions to such a degree we will not have room enough to receive it. I'd like to contend that point. Money is a containable commodity. If I had all the money in the world I could contain it. So what is God speaking of when He states we will not be able to contain the reward of giving? The answer is found in Proverbs:

> "Honor the LORD with your possessions (these are your gifts to ministers or offerings for ministries), and with the first-fruits of all your increase (this is your tithe); so your barns will be filled with plenty, and your vats will *overflow* with new wine."
>
> —3:9–10 (words in parentheses and italics are mine)

Your barns represent your storage places. That would be your checkbook, closets, gas tanks, garage, etc. This is where we store our containable commodities. So it is true, He blesses our finances. However, what is the blessing which we will not have room to receive? The answer is found as we continue to read: "your vats will overflow with new wine." A vat is a large container used to store wine. Notice in this scripture, this is what cannot contain the blessing of God, for He states they will *overflow*. What does new wine represent? In the Bible new wine always represents the fresh presence of the Holy Spirit. God is saying when you honor Him, by giving to church leaders—giving to their churches or ministries, you will receive the full reward of the overflow of His presence! That is the most exciting promise of all.

Time and time again, I've witnessed those who are generous in financially honoring their spiritual leaders are those who are blessed materially, and have enough to do every good work that comes before them. But it goes further. What I've also observed is they walk in an overflow of God's presence. Why should this surprise us—it's God's promise? Understanding this truth answered my question of why I couldn't sense a strong presence of God in meetings where honor was withheld—where the pastor was struggling, or where I'm treated like a common traveler. The people were not generous. However, once they became liberal and continued to do so, the presence of God was so much stronger in their church.

If you take the truths of this chapter and read the entire Bible, you'll notice whenever the people of God richly gave, miracles, freedom, salvations, God's presence, and prosperity would abound. We cannot buy the blessings of God; however, it is a spiritual principle God has weaved into His grace. Hear what Paul said of the Macedonian believers: "And now, brothers, we want you to know about the grace that God has given the Macedonian churches. Out of the most severe trial, their overflowing joy and their extreme poverty welled up in rich generosity. For I testify that they gave as much as they were able, and even beyond their ability" (2 Cor. 8:1–3, NIV).

Paul attributed their generosity as a direct result of the grace of God. God's grace gave them the capacity to go "beyond their ability." Just as we can't buy grace, we also can't buy favor, but we certainly can position ourselves to receive it. By giving double financial honor to those who bring the Word of God to us, we position ourselves to be honored by God; included in that honor is grace and favor—it's a spiritual law.

CHAPTER 12

Honoring Our Peers

He who honors you honors Me, and he who honors
Me honors Him who sent Me. He who honors a
prophet in the name of a prophet shall receive a prophet's
reward. And he who honors a righteous man in the name
of a righteous man shall receive a righteous man's reward.
And whoever honors one of these little ones with only a
cup of cold water in the name of a disciple, assuredly, I
say to you, he shall by no means lose his reward.

—MATTHEW 10:40–42 (AUTHOR'S PARAPHRASE)

❦

Now we turn from those who are over us in authority to those who are on our level. We're neither over them, nor they over us. This is identified by the second group Jesus speaks of: "he who *honors* a righteous man in the name of a righteous man shall receive a righteous man's reward."

A Double Reward

Allow me to first start off with a testimony which exemplifies honoring on this level. For several years I've taken my family on a yearly cruise. Our children have never complained about Lisa's and my immense travels to bring the Word of God to people globally.

They've been not only supportive but enthusiastic about our calling. We love God's provision for us to reward them with this special vacation at the close of each year. Our boys enjoy cruises because we can't be reached by cell phone, or send and receive emails. We have the agreement that our computers stay off the entire week, no work. We're all theirs for the week.

A few years back we'd just finished the cruise. I called our director of staff and he reported some very disappointing news. While we were on the vacation, a pastor I knew in our city hired one of our key employees out from under us. This employee was responsible for all international rights for our book translations. Her position took considerable training and knowledge seeing she worked with publishers globally. Developing a rapport and relationship with them was crucial and took time.

To say I was upset is an understatement. I fought hard feelings toward this pastor. We'd spent nine months training her, and he didn't give me the courtesy of a call to see how it would affect our organization in hiring her away. I could understand his move more if he was not saved and working in the secular world, but for a minister to hire away from another ministry without first discussing it leader to leader just didn't make Kingdom sense. Besides that, he was a friend.

For a couple days I worked through the angry feelings in prayer. How would we find another so quickly to replace her? I dreaded the lost time to retrain a new person. I fought against critical thoughts. I longed to make sense of what he'd done, but there was no logic. How could he be so insensitive? After two or three days the Lord spoke to me while in prayer, "Son, I want you to give him your new watch."

While on the cruise, in a shop in Jamaica, I found a neat watch. It was a brand-new eco-drive Citizens brand, which looked really good. I hadn't bought a watch in a few years and was excited about its new sleek design.

Once God spoke to me, it didn't take long to perceive His wisdom. He was giving me the opportunity to release any wrong thoughts I was developing in my heart toward this pastor, and replace them with honor. He was protecting me from harboring an offense, and guarding my relationship with both Himself and the pastor. In prayer I started smiling, and eventually laughing. I was amazed at both the wisdom and love of my Father. He was moving on behalf of both His sons. I said yes enthusiastically to His request, and immediately all the anger and resentment for what the pastor did drained out of my system. It was a quick deliverance. Now I found myself excited to give something I valued to my brother in Christ.

The next evening we talked on the phone. I was now ready to converse since the resentment was gone. It turned out he made a careless mistake. He confessed he just didn't think it through, and was very apologetic. He now understood, due to the confrontation, his course of action was wrong. However, had God not dealt with my heart beforehand, it could have been an ugly and damaging phone call. My tone of voice and attitude could have sparked a fire of problems in our relationship.

At this point let me say this: confrontation is good, however it must be done with a right heart attitude. It must be done for the sake of the other person, not for us. I did share why the way he went about it was wrong, but it was bathed in genuine love for him, which made it easy for him to receive what I said. After our conversation I asked if I could come by his office. He agreed, and we set a time.

When I arrived he was curious. We had already brought closure to the matter; he wondered about the reason for my visit. I shared my desire to give him the watch. Overwhelmed he said, "John, I need a watch, I don't have one." I was so blessed to discover this. I took the watch out of the box and he tried it on. It didn't fit because my wrist is smaller than his. The problem was we'd left the spare links in the jewelry shop in Jamaica. I told him I'd order more from the company. He tried to talk me into letting him do it, but I didn't want to give an incomplete gift.

Since that time we've become much closer than we've ever been. We both have a great deal of respect for each other. It thrills my heart to know he wears the watch. I enjoy seeing it on him far more than on me. I've seen our former employee several times since, and I'm always thrilled to see her progress.

However, I was still faced with the fact we had the void on our staff, but I knew God would take care of us. I'd acted in such a way that would keep the door open for His provision.

Now let me share the reward of honor. A few weeks later our human resources person hired a woman named Darcie to replace our previous international rights lady. The way I describe Darcie is as a human tiger. I've seen very few in the past who possess such passion to see the Word of God get into the hands of believers globally. She came aboard hitting the ground running. Our other employees in this position used to wait for things to happen; not Darcie, she would pray, and then go after international publishers to print our books.

The previous lady did a good job. In nine months she took our translations from eighteen to twenty-three languages. Darcie, in her first nine months, brought our translations from twenty-three to forty! Yes, you read it right. The other lady grew our books into five new languages; Darcie did over three times as much, seventeen new languages, in the same amount of time. At the time of this writing we are now at forty-five languages, thanks to the grace of God upon Darcie's life.

I don't believe this would have happened had I not honored the pastor who hired our lady out from under us. We received a reward; the Word of God we steward is touching far more lives. Some of the accomplishments she's made are getting our books, by the tens of thousands, into leaders' hands in places of the world hostile to the gospel. In fact, some of the areas they've been placed I can't even share with our ministry partners, for the sake of protecting the leaders in these persecuting nations.

I can think of no greater reward than the ability to touch many more lives with the Word of God. However, God wasn't finished. There was still another reward coming of which I was completely unaware. A few months later I was in a city speaking on a Sunday morning. After the service the pastor took me to lunch. A businessman was invited to join us. While in the men's bathroom of the restaurant, the businessman asked, "John, what kind of watch would you like to have?"

Needless to say, I was caught a bit off guard by his question. I stuttered a bit and finally said, "You don't want to know."

He insisted, "No, John, I really do want to know. What kind of watch would you like to have?"

In seeing his persistence I proceeded to say, "For the past several years my dream watch is a Breitling."

Breitling watches are made by a division of Bentley Motor Company. They are very expensive and hard to find; you can't find them in every city. I admired one on a man's wrist years earlier. The design appealed to my eye, and I thought how nice it would be to have one. I enjoy flying (even though I'm not a pilot), and it was originally made for pilots. We eventually found a shop that carried them in a large city. Lisa and I were a bit taken aback by the price, and I determined not to spend that kind of money on a watch, but I still liked them.

Upon hearing my reply, the businessman pushed up his coat sleeve and took a recently purchased, top-of-the-line Breitling Navitimer watch off his wrist. He then put it on my wrist and said with a smile, "John, while you were speaking in service this morning God told me to give you this watch."

I about came unglued, but at the same time was speechless and overwhelmed. He could never have known, without God telling him, a Breitling was my favorite watch; and to make it even sweeter, top-of-the-line aviator style. What were the chances of him having this watch on his wrist?

A few hours after the initial shock of receiving the watch, the thought came to me of how I gave my brand-new watch to honor the pastor a few months back. I now realized God was doing what He said He would do—honoring me in return. For remember He states, "For those who honor Me I will honor" (1 Sam. 2:30). You may say, "But John, you didn't honor God, you honored the pastor." Remember Jesus says, "He who honors My servant, honors Me, and He who honors Me honors the Father" (Matt. 10:40, author's paraphrase).

Every time I look at the watch—and it is on my wrist now as I write—I see it as a beautiful gift from my Father. It means far more to me than had I gone out and bought it myself. It also means far more to me than if this man just gave me an expensive watch as a gift. It's not the watch, but the sentiment behind it, which means so much. God will do the same, but in different ways, to all those who honor Him, by honoring His servants.

Love Coupled with Holy Fear

I hope by now it's coming into clear view: to honor is to genuinely love. It takes both holy fear and unconditional love to walk in true honor. We are told,

> "Let love be without hypocrisy. Abhor what is evil. Cling to what is good. Be kindly affectionate to one another with brotherly love, in honor giving preference to one another."
>
> —Rom. 12:9–10

There is so much in these two verses. First of all, Paul states true love has no hypocrisy. A definition of *hypocrisy* is "the concealment of one's real character or motives" (*Webster's*, 1828). This would be characterized by one who acts as though they honor by their outward actions and words, but within they criticize, envy, or even despise you. Or in your absence, they cut down, defame, or slander you. In the southern part of the United States a culture has been developed that could easily lead to this. We've all heard of southern hospitality, a gentleman of the South, or a southern belle. All of these terms imply that those of this part of the country are given to graciousness and honor. Yet what's happened with some brought up this way is they've learned to live up to this expectation in pretense, rather than in truth.

In times past I've witnessed a few individuals in the South who will speak crudely of others in their absence, later only to find them speaking and treating the very same people with an appearance of great honor, love, and respect. On the other hand, other parts of the country are different; people don't have this expectation to live up to, so they tend to be more straightforward. In particular I get a kick out of the people in the Northeast. It's common that if they don't like you, they'll tell you to your face. They've not been trained in pretense; rather they are usually matter-of-fact, or better put, blunt.

To extend true honor, it must be done without hypocrisy. It can never be done in pretense; it'll only lead to deception, and there's definitely no reward for the counterfeit. Paul continues in this vein: "Let love be without hypocrisy. Abhor what is evil. Cling to what is good." To abhor evil and cling to what is good is the fear of the Lord. Proverbs 8:13 states, "The fear of the LORD is to hate evil." The fear of the Lord keeps us from deception. It keeps us from blinding ourselves to a hypocritical behavior. Let's again examine God's correction in this. Isaiah states, "Because this people draw near with their words and honor Me with their lip service, but they remove their hearts far from Me, and their reverence for Me consists of tradition learned by rote" (Isa. 29:13, NASB).

The word *rote* is defined as "frequent repetition of words or sounds, without attending to the signification, or to principles." God states the people show honor with their mouths, and in other parts of the book of Isaiah with their actions, but their hearts are not in it. It's honor with hypocrisy, which is no honor at all. Why are they given to this behavior? Because of the absence of the fear of the Lord, "their reverence for Me" consists of routine; something that has just become habit.

This is seen so often within church circles. We are so focused on being polite; we lose sight of speaking from our hearts. Let me give an example. Steve is hurrying to a meeting. He's five minutes late and it's crucial to be on time. As he's walking down the busy street he catches a glimpse of Jim, a brother from church he's not seen in weeks, walking the opposite way on the other side of the street. He thinks, *Oh no, I hope Jim doesn't see me. I just don't have time to talk, nor is he one of my favorite people.*

All of a sudden Jim and Steve catch eyes, and Jim immediately starts across the street to greet his brother in Christ. Steve now realizes he has to acknowledge Jim, or he would be taken for rude. So Steve heads toward his Christian brother who is crossing the street to meet him. Steve speaks first because he's in a hurry and needs to get this interaction over with: "Jim, praise God, it's great to see you."

Jim returns the greeting and asks how Steve is doing.

Steve says, "Oh just great, but you know I'm late for a meeting, so why don't I call you and we'll get together for lunch sometime." The two part ways.

Let's go over Steve's brief conversation with Jim. First of all he says, "Praise God, it's great to see you." Steve wasn't even thinking of God at that moment; it is just a routine he's built into his speech to *show* excitement and his faith when seeing a fellow Christian. Second, it was not great to see Jim; he was hoping Jim wouldn't notice him. So in just the first statement he's yielded to deception and lying, without a hint of conviction.

Then Steve's closing remark is, "Why don't I call you and we'll get together for lunch sometime." He has no intention of calling Jim and getting together for lunch. It is just his way of getting out of the uncomfortable situation he's found himself in. Another lie.

Would Steve lie on purpose? Most likely he wouldn't. Why isn't he collapsing under conviction? Because he's learned to love in pretense because of the lack of the fear of the Lord in his life. This leads him to a lifestyle by rote, which shows love and honor, when in reality it's just a hollow form of love.

The fear of the Lord keeps us aware of the fact God knows in detail every thought and intent, along with every word we speak. Even idle words we will give an account of on the Day of Judgment (see Matt. 12:36). We read, "Come, you children, listen to me; I will teach you the fear of the LORD. . . . Keep your tongue from evil, and your lips from speaking deceit. Depart from evil and do good" (Ps. 34:11, 13–14).

Oh, how we must love in truth, and this can only be done by passionately desiring and walking in the fear of the Lord! How terrible to be deceived, to live in pretense; only Godly fear can keep us from this trap.

Esteeming the Other Better

In Romans Paul continues, "Be kindly affectionate to one another with brotherly love, in honor giving preference to one another" (12:10). Honor gives preference to others because it values and esteems them. Paul again says this in another letter:

> Therefore if *there is* any consolation in Christ, if any comfort of love, if any fellowship of the Spirit, if any affection and mercy, fulfill my joy by being like-minded, having the

same love, *being* of one accord, of one mind. *Let* nothing *be done* through selfish ambition or conceit, but in lowliness of mind let each esteem others better than himself. Let each of you look out not only for his own interests, but also for the interests of others. Let this mind be in you which was also in Christ Jesus.

—Philippians 2:1–5

To esteem others better than yourself is to honor them. We should ponder, meditate, and prayerfully consider these words in all our life activities and affairs. If we would learn this, getting it deeply rooted in our beings, we would walk in great blessing, as it is true honor.

Notice Paul says, "Let this mind be in you which was also in Christ Jesus." I'll never forget the words the Lord spoke to me when I was a very young Christian. I was driving in my car and I heard Him say, "John, do you know I esteem you better than Myself?"

Alarmed by hearing these words, I was in shock thinking it had to be the enemy trying to sow a blasphemous or prideful thought into my being. How could the One who made the universe and all that is within it, tell me, a little peon of a person, He considered me more valuable than Himself? I almost said, "Get behind me, Satan, you are an offense to me." But somehow deep in my spirit I knew it was the voice of Jesus. I still had to be sure, for I knew at a young spiritual age the Word of God commands us to "test the spirits" (1 John 4:1).

I collected my thoughts and replied, "Lord, I just cannot believe this unless You give me three witnesses from the New Testament." I was trembling speaking these words, but I knew it was the right thing to do.

I sensed in my heart the Lord had no contention with my request; in fact I felt His pleasure in my asking. I heard Him say almost immediately, "What does Philippians 2:3 say?"

I knew it by heart so I recited it aloud back to Him: "Let nothing be done through selfish ambition or conceit, but in lowliness of mind let each esteem others better than himself."

The Lord replied, "There is your first witness."

I quickly countered, "No, Lord, that wasn't what Paul was saying. He was telling the Philippian believers to esteem each other better than themselves; he was not writing in regard to how You treat and esteem me."

The Lord immediately said to me, "I don't tell My children to do anything that I don't do Myself!"

I was taken back.

He then said, "That is the problem with so many families. The parents tell their children to do things they don't do, or they tell them to not do things they do. Many parents tell their children not to fight and yet they fight in front of them continuously. Then the parents wonder why their children fight. I don't do this."

I was still a little leery, so I said, "That is only one scripture, I still need two others."

I then heard, "Who died on the cross, you or Me?"

I was stunned.

I then heard, "I hung on that cross bearing your sins, sickness, diseases, poverty, and judgment, because I esteemed you better than Myself." (The scripture reference He gave me was 1 Pet. 2:24.)

I now realized I had surely heard the voice of the Lord. He did honor (esteem) me more than Himself, otherwise He would not have taken my judgment and died in my place. I knew a third scripture was on the way, and without having to ask I heard in my heart, "The third witness is, 'Be kindly affectionate to one another with brotherly love, in honor giving preference to one another'" (Rom. 12:10). He then spoke to my heart, "I am the firstborn of many brothers [see Rom. 8:29], and in honor I esteem My brothers and sisters better than Myself."

Of course this applies to every child of God, not just me. He literally esteems each of us in honor better than Himself. That's almost too wonderful to comprehend. It's the true love of God.

You may say, "But John, that is Jesus Christ. We could never love like that." Well here is the amazing fact—we actually can. We are told the Holy Spirit has placed the love of God in our hearts (see Rom. 5:5). The evidence is found in Paul's own words. Listen to what he said in regard to his fellow countrymen:

> In the presence of Christ, I speak with utter truthfulness—I do not lie—and my conscience and the Holy Spirit confirm that what I am saying is true. My heart is filled with bitter sorrow and unending grief for my people, my Jewish brothers and sisters. I would be willing to be forever cursed—cut off from Christ!—if that would save them.
>
> —Romans 9:1–3 (NLT)

I still shudder at these words of Paul's. He is saying, and it is definitely not written in pretense, that he would be willing to be cut off from Christ, salvation, for all eternity in order to see his fellow countrymen and women saved. How could a mere man walk in that kind of love and honor? It's impossible to do through human love; only the love of God, which motivated Jesus, could honor in such a way. Paul developed that love and honor so strong within his heart it resulted in this cry coming forth. And let me further say this: the Holy Spirit would have never allowed him to pen these words, unless he really meant it. You cannot lie—write deception—when penning the Scripture.

Do you see the potential in all of us who are born again? Romans 5:5 emphatically states, "For God's love has been poured out in our hearts through the Holy Spirit Who has been given to us" (AMP). This is why Jesus tells us, "A new commandment I give to you, that you love one another; as I have loved you, that you also love one another" (John 13:34). It was a new commandment because people couldn't walk in that kind of love in the Old Testament. The love of God had not yet been poured out into their hearts. Notice the words "as I have loved you." He gave Himself for us completely, He was separated from the Father, He cried, "My God, My God, why have you forsaken Me?" (Matt. 27:46). He willingly chose to become poor, separated from God, so we could have eternal life. He honored us to the highest level, and Paul was able to honestly say the same words in regard to his countrymen. Oh Father, help us to walk in this manner of love! You've given us the potential; now we need to develop it in cooperation with the Holy Spirit.

That, my dear brothers and sisters, is true honor: we esteem our fellow believers, and those who need Jesus, as valuable, weighty, and precious. This will motivate us to give to the work of the Kingdom in every way, be it service, prayer, or finances. It will motivate us to do what the Macedonians did. Their honor was Christlike, and Paul used their love to motivate the Corinthian believers:

> My friends, we want you to know that the churches in Macedonia have shown others how kind God is. Although they were going through hard times and were very poor, they were glad to give generously. They gave as much as they could afford and even more, simply because they wanted to. They even asked and begged us to let them have the joy of giving their money for God's people. And they did more than we had hoped. They gave themselves first to the Lord and then to us, just as God wanted them to do.
>
> Titus was the one who got you started doing this good thing, so we begged him to have you finish what you had begun. You do everything better than anyone else. You have

stronger faith. You speak better and know more. You are eager to give, and you love us better. Now you must give more generously than anyone else.

I am not ordering you to do this. I am simply testing how real your love is by comparing it with the concern that others have shown. You know that our Lord Jesus Christ was kind enough to give up all his riches and become poor, so that you could become rich.

A year ago you were the first ones to give, and you gave because you wanted to. So listen to my advice. I think you should finish what you started. If you give according to what you have, you will prove that you are as eager to give as you were to think about giving. It doesn't matter how much you have. What matters is how much you are willing to give from what you have.

I am not trying to make life easier for others by making life harder for you. But it is only fair for you to share with them when you have so much, and they have so little.

—2 Corinthians 8:1–14 (CEV)

Paul was using the honor the Macedonians extended to those in need to urge the believers of Corinth to live out the love God has placed in all believers. It's there—the love of God is in our hearts. We must cooperate with the Holy Spirit to develop it. Don't say, "Well, that's not my personality or the way I am." This will only hinder you from walking in a way that will bring true fulfillment to your heart, joy to those you influence, and a great reward not only in this life but especially in the one to come. Don't hold back; honor your fellow believers. You'll be glad you did throughout eternity.

CHAPTER 13

Honoring Those Entrusted to Us

He who honors *you* honors *Me, and he who* honors
Me honors *Him who sent Me. He who* honors *a*
prophet in the name of a prophet shall receive a prophet's
reward. And he who honors *a righteous man in the name*
of a righteous man shall receive a righteous man's reward.
And whoever honors *one of these little ones with only a*
cup of cold water in the name of a disciple, assuredly, I say
to you, he shall by no means lose his reward.

—MATTHEW 10:40–42 (AUTHOR'S PARAPHRASE)

❧

Now we turn to those who are entrusted to us—persons under our authority. This group is identified by Jesus' words, "And whoever *honors* one of these little ones with only a cup of cold water in the name of a disciple, assuredly, I say to you, he shall by no means lose his reward."

Little Ones

In Scripture "little ones" are identified as small children or those entrusted to our delegated authority. We'll focus on the latter, which in a family setting would be our children. Many little ones have been mistreated and even abused by those in authority. This angers the heart of God, for Jesus in no uncertain terms warns,

It will be terrible for people who cause even one of my little followers to sin. Those people would be better off thrown into the deepest part of the ocean with a heavy stone tied around their necks! The world is in for trouble because of the way it causes people to sin. There will always be something to cause people to sin, but anyone who does this will be in for trouble. . . . Don't be cruel to any of these little ones! I promise you that their angels are always with my Father in heaven.

—Matthew 18:6–7,10 (CEV)

That's a sobering warning. When Jesus says *terrible*, you better believe it will indeed be *terrible*. Why is He so stern? God is the One who delegates authority; He is love, and releases His authority for the purpose of love and protection. If it's instead used to abuse, take advantage of, or harm the little ones, it becomes a direct affront to Him. You may think, *It's not a direct affront to Him, but rather His people.* That's not so, for Jesus says, "Assuredly, I say to you, inasmuch as you did it to one of the *least of these* My brethren, you did it to Me" (Matt. 25:40, emphasis mine). How we treat those under us is how we treat Jesus. Consider this in the way you handle your children, spouse, employees, students, and so forth.

Those entrusted with authority have the responsibility to correct and discipline. Some leaders cause little ones to stumble by neglecting to correct when it's needed. A child left to himself will end up corrupt rather than healthy. Paul shows the importance of godly discipline in his letter to the Corinthians: "You may think I overstate the authority He gave me, but I'm not backing off. Every bit of my commitment is for the purpose of building you up, after all, not tearing you down" (2 Cor. 10:8, The Message). In reading the two letters written to the Corinthians, it's not difficult to detect the firmness of Paul's discipline toward them. He valued these little ones by bringing correction and training. However, he clearly states authority is given for the purpose of building up, which would include serving and protecting. You as the leader must ask yourself, *Is this my motive?* If you honor little ones, it will be your motive; therefore you'll correct when needed.

On the other end of the spectrum, others do the opposite. These I speak of cause little ones to stumble by using their authority for selfish purposes. Their correction is damaging. They have not developed love in their hearts, through prayer and mediation, for those under their care. Our hearts should burn to see those entrusted to us prosper. Will they make mistakes? Of course. Just remember when you were young and immature, or have you so quickly forgotten? I was a challenge to those who were over me. I made stupid mistakes and sinned. I was impulsive, moved without thinking things through, and made ignorant and ridiculous statements, especially at the wrong time. I'm so grateful my leaders didn't give up on me.

I recall years ago when my wife and I were initially building our staff. We had a handful of employees (at the time of this writing we have over fifty). We were troubled by their mistakes. I remember making a comment to Lisa that I believe was a prophetic word that would bring correction and understanding to both of us. I said, "Lisa, if the people God places under us don't need anything from us, why would God place them under our authority?" We both nodded in affirmation.

Church Leadership

In traveling to thousands of churches over the years, I've been exposed to a variety of leadership. I'm particularly excited about leaders who think creatively. They're building the house of God in unconventional ways. Our methods are becoming friendlier to those who are not saved. Atmospheres are developed making unbelievers feel welcomed, rather than old traditional settings, which are foreign to the unchurched. We're getting rid of the formal attire, the twenty-year-old songs, and the church lingo, and we're using multimedia to replace what used to be the mundane way of communicating announcements or events, and this is just to name a few. I personally believe this is the wisdom of God.

As a side note, always remember, God is for seeker-sensitive methods, however, He is against seeker-sensitive messages. In regard to seeker-sensitive messages Paul clearly states, "Do I seek to please men? For if I still pleased men, I would not be a bond-servant of Christ" (Gal. 1:10). We should never communicate a compromised gospel in order to reach more people. If we do so, we will build a congregation of counterfeit disciples who risk hearing the words from Jesus on that great day: "Depart from Me, I never knew you," (see Matt. 7:20–23). Their blood will be on our hands. Paul informed a group of leaders, "I am innocent of the blood of all men. For I have not shunned to declare to you the whole counsel of God" (Acts 20:26–27). We cannot just proclaim selected positive segments from Scripture; we must also warn and correct (see Col. 1:28).

Jesus clearly tells us the Holy Spirit will "convict the world of sin" (John 16:8). A congregation that doesn't bring conviction to those living in sin due to its seeker-friendly messages is no different than the Laodicean church found in the book of Revelations. This assembly was on the verge of being vomited out of Jesus, for they would not allow Him to bring godly purification through the presence of His Holy Spirit. Consequently He pleaded with this church, "Behold, I stand at the door and knock" (Rev. 3:20). This shows the extreme danger of seeker-sensitive messages.

However, in regard to seeker-sensitive methods Paul says,

Even though I am free of the demands and expectations of everyone, I have voluntarily become a servant to any and all in order to reach a wide range of people: religious, non-religious, meticulous moralists, loose-living immoralists, the defeated, the demoralized—whoever. I didn't take on their way of life. I kept my bearings in Christ—but I entered their world and tried to experience things from their point of view. I've become just about every sort of servant there is in my attempts to lead those I meet into a God-saved life.

—1 Corinthians 9:19–22 (The Message)

Hear his words, "I entered their world and tried to experience things from their point of view." In speaking recently to hundreds of pastors I pleaded with them to walk into their own service as a visitor and experience it from an unchurched person's point of view. I then said, "If you're honest and open, many of you will be making numerous changes."

In the body of Christ we should be on the cutting edge of communication and technology. The world should be inspired by our creativity and innovation. Why should the secular arenas possess excellence and the kingdom of God be represented by second-class operations? No, just as Daniel and the other Hebrews were wiser than the sons of the greatest kingdom of the world, we too should be sought out for our innovative ideas.

Let's proclaim and teach the Word of God in the power of the Holy Spirit without any compromise, but package it in such a way it can be assimilated by the unchurched. Our message must bring strong heart conviction to the disobedient and unsaved. We must call for complete submission to Christ Jesus, which means repentance from sin, ungodliness, and worldly desires, coupled with the giving of 100 percent our lives to follow Him. We can do this with joy in our lives and messages coupled with innovative ideas. To be a Christian doesn't mean we lose enthusiasm and creativity. No, rather in Christ we find these qualities in abundance. If we honor the little ones, we will spend the time to think creatively on their behalf. This pleases the heart of God.

Life Enhancing or Draining

Now hear what Peter says to the leaders of the church:

> I warn *and* counsel the elders among you (the pastors and spiritual guides of the church) as a fellow elder. . . . Tend (nurture, guard, guide, and fold) the flock of God that is [your responsibility], not by coercion *or* constraint, but willingly; not dishonorably motivated by the advantages *and* profits [belonging to the office], but eagerly *and* cheerfully; not domineering [as arrogant, dictatorial, and overbearing persons] over those in your charge, but being examples (patterns and models of Christian living) to the flock (the congregation).
>
> —1 Peter 5:1–3 (AMP)

You can use many different terms to describe the variety of leadership styles found within the twenty-first-century church: traditional, progressive, legalistic, team building, dictatorial, empowering, micromanaging, and the list continues. However, you can narrow this extensive list down to two main categories: life enhancing and life draining. The difference is found in the heart of the leader.

Some leaders can get much accomplished outwardly, but leave bruised, wounded, and even dead followers behind them. On the other hand, others also accomplish much, but all the while edify those they lead. Much of it comes down to honor or dishonor in the heart of the leader.

Men and women who are visionaries can approach the building of ministry one of two ways. The dishonoring leader, who causes the little ones to stumble, sees the people as vehicles to serve his or her vision. The true leader, who builds lives, sees his or her vision as the vehicle to serve the people. This leader honors those entrusted to their care. It's amazing how this heart motive will produce such different results in the people. Jesus says, "Wisdom is shown to be right by what results from it" (Matt. 11:19, NLT). I've seen emotionally battered people in congregations (happy to say it's rare), while in other churches I've witnessed healthy individuals and families. It all revolves around honor.

The honoring leader will encourage the development of people. His or her greatest joy will be to see those entrusted to their care walking in intimacy with God and flourishing in their life callings. The combination of these two major aspects of the Christian life comprises walking in truth. See John's words concerning the people placed under his care: "For I rejoiced greatly when brethren came and testified of the truth that is in you, just as you walk in the truth. I have no greater joy than to hear that my children walk in truth" (3 John 1:3–4).

To walk in truth is to both know and serve God. Jesus says on the Judgment Day there will be people who did great works in His name, but He will declare, "Depart from Me, I never knew you." They missed the most important aspect of salvation—to intimately know God. Good leaders will stress relationship with God.

Then there'll be others who, though they knew God, greatly displeased Him. They were entrusted with gifts to fulfill their role in building His house, but neglected their responsibility. On that day the Master will say to those who buried their talents, "You wicked and lazy servant!" (Matt. 25:26, NLT).

Every believer has a calling to build the house of God. Ephesians 2:10 clearly states that "we are His workmanship, created in Christ Jesus for good works, which God prepared beforehand that we should walk in them." We were created not only to be someone but to do something. It's tragic when people get off balance with their teaching. I've heard preachers make statements such as, "It's not what we do, but who we are; we are not human doings, but human beings." It's a cute play on words, but an unbalanced portrayal of the Christian life. We do cease from our own labors when we become believers. However, Scripture shows once saved we then enter His labor. We are to bear fruit, and this is proof that our faith is genuine (see James 2). This teaching, which emphasizes who we are to the neglect of what we're called to do, encourages people to attend church once a week, but refrain from getting planted and active in the house of God. The believers developed by this manner of teaching will not have pleasant experiences at the Judgment. We were created in Christ Jesus to accomplish specific works; these works were planned before we were created in our mother's womb; we'll give an account for our responsibility that was prepared beforehand (see Ps. 139:16).

The honoring leader's goal is to see the little ones walk in truth, and to go further. True fathers and mothers desire their children to surpass their own success. Jesus stated His desire for us: to do greater works than He did. We should have the same heart for those who follow us. Leaders should burn in their hearts to see this for those who are under them, as John spoke in his letter. It should be one of our greatest joys.

Think on These Things

The wise long-term leaders are the ones who continually pass the credit for his or her success to those who serve them. (Of course, all credit, honor, thanksgiving and glory go to God, but we must remember God uses people.) The leader displays his or her honor toward the team members by praising their efforts. This is something that is done not superficially, but from the heart. As a leader I try to always think highly of those who help accomplish our mission; they are gifts from heaven. I guard myself from negative thoughts toward our employees. In doing so I maintain honor for them within my heart. Paul tells us,

> Brethren, whatever is true, whatever is worthy of reverence *and* is honorable *and* seemly, whatever is just, whatever is pure, whatever is lovely *and* lovable, whatever is kind *and* winsome *and* gracious, if there is any virtue *and* excellence, if there is anything worthy of praise, think on *and* weigh *and* take account of these things [fix your minds on them].
>
> —Philippians 4:8 (AMP)

I recall a time in our marriage when I was disillusioned with Lisa. To be frank, I was not happy with her at all. My poor attitude had been building for months. It was not getting better, but worse. At one point during a disagreement I just walked out the door and headed to a field. I didn't want to be anywhere near her. I griped about Lisa to myself and to the Lord all the way out to the field. Once I arrived, I heard clearly in my heart, "Son, I want you to think of the things Lisa does well, and thank Me for them."

Of course, at the moment I wasn't the least bit positive. However, I was able to think of one aspect: her being a good mother. However, in my frustration, I didn't think there would be many more attributes to name. Once I thanked God for her being a great mother, another aspect came to mind; once I thanked God for that area of her life, another came to mind. This continued for quite some time, and eventually I found myself overwhelmed by what an amazing wife I had. Something interesting happened: I started seeing our situation from a much different perspective; this caused me to realize I'd been a very poor husband for the entire time period I was disillusioned with her. I had truly come to my senses and was now seeing things accurately. It was a God's-eye view.

I came back to our house and started telling her of all the attributes I appreciated, and I just kept going and going. On and on I went; it was flowing out of my heart. When I left for the field she appeared so angry it would have taken quite some time to restore our fellowship. However, because I was honoring her from my heart, and it just kept pouring out of me, it brought immediate reconciliation. From that day forward we saw healing and restoration come into our marriage, and it's never regressed to where it was at that time.

The same thing will happen with our children, employees, students, and church members if we just do what Philippians 4:8 instructs us to do. Think of the lovely, good, and pleasant, in regard to those under our care. Think of how valuable they are to our Father; they are His sons and daughters. If they're not saved, focus on the fact they were worth Jesus dying for. If we'll do this we will guard our heart from dishonor. We will be blessed.

Again, this doesn't mean we refrain from correction when it's needed. However, when it comes to correction we do it concisely and effectively. Our children and employees know we don't carry grudges. They've commented that we can be stern, but once the correction is complete we joke or laugh with them shortly afterward. I've learned this lesson from God Himself. Once we are disciplined by Him, and respond to it, our Father is quick to forgive and forget. He doesn't carry grudges. He doesn't leave a trail of shame to accompany us; only the enemy does this—rather He buries our errors in the sea of forgetfulness. All He asks of us is to learn from His correction so we don't have to make the same mistake again. Our Father's thoughts of love, honor, and hope toward us are so numerous they outnumber all the grains of sand the earth contains (see Ps. 139).

When the leader honors the little ones, it in turn releases the gift of God in their lives. As their gift flourishes the leader in turn benefits as his or her vision is accomplished through all the gifts of the people combined in the organization. I'm amazed by some pastors I've run across who speak down to their staff. They speak in harsh, demanding tones and communicate to their people as if they were stupid. Then I've heard these same leaders make the comment, "I just can't find competent people. I need better employees." No wonder. They don't value their people; therefore they're receiving no reward due to dishonor.

Financially

Just as we honor leaders with our finances, so we honor little ones in the same way. A few years ago, I was helping Lisa's assistant with her personal finances. We were setting up her monthly budget. At that time we paid our employees the standard rates established by ministries in Colorado Springs. I added up her expenses and noticed things were tight. I blurted out, "You can't live decently off this salary." My wife, who was standing by, heartily agreed.

I immediately jumped on the phone to our chief financial officer. I said, "I just got done helping Lisa's assistant with her budget. We don't pay her enough. No one on our staff should live off income this low. I want all our employees raised up to this level [I stated the figure] of yearly salary. I don't care if they are mailing out packages or answering phones."

The phone line went quiet for a moment, then our CFO said, "If you do this, you'll be one of the most-sought-out ministries in our city to work for."

I replied, "That's not the reason I'm doing it. Our team members give their lives to serve God with us; they need to be compensated well."

A good number of our staff received large raises that day. It came as a total surprise, and they were grateful to hear the news. One young lady was planning to turn in her resignation that very week. She planned to move back to her family in Indiana; her financial situation had become too difficult. That day she received an annual five-thousand-dollar raise. She didn't resign.

Now, years later, she is still with us and has been promoted to supervisor of a department. She is one of our most productive and valued employees. I've seen her grow leaps and bounds. I shudder to think what would have happened had she departed due to finances.

Our reward didn't just manifest with this lady; we saw it ministry wide. It seemed the productivity of the staff as a whole increased from that time forward. We entered into a new level of effectiveness. We honored our employees, which resulted in the reward of greater productivity.

A note of caution here. As I've stated earlier it opposes the heart of God to demand honor. We should desire honor for two reasons: first, so we can pass it on to God in our heart, and second for the sake of the one who gives it, knowing they'll receive a reward. In my early days of ministry I worked for a large church as an associate pastor. We were paid a minimal salary. Our total income per month was equivalent to our living expenses, with nothing extra left over for clothes or furniture. We agreed to this salary; it's what was offered to us. We didn't want to be demanding hirelings.

After the first year, no raise was offered. After two years, still no raise. We now had two children instead of one. The cost of living was increasing, and we were still at the same level as the day we started.

One of the other associate pastors, a friend, came into my office a few times over the course of those two years and asked me to join with some other assistant pastors in approaching the administrator and senior pastor for a raise.

My reply was that I would have no part in it, and I recommended he not do it as well. "It is not my place to tell them how to honor me," I told him.

My friend countered, "John, my wife and I have to get support from our family to live. My parents are sending us money to make ends meet."

I told him how sorry I was to learn this, but that I would continue to trust God. I tried to minister faith to him, by explaining that God was our source, not the paycheck. It didn't seem to get through.

I can't say my family was not under pressure, because we were, but we had peace and never lacked in those years. We had very little furniture in our house: a bed frame, without the headboard, two small love seats, a few end tables and lamps, and a kitchen table and chairs was all we had on the bottom floor. However, in just one year we saw God miraculously fill our home with furniture, and much of it was nice designer and custom-made pieces. We were in awe of God's provision.

A little over two years later our pastor launched us into the traveling ministry. We would no longer receive a paycheck. We had three hundred dollars in savings and still had a house and car payment that totaled a thousand dollars a month. To make matters more interesting, the Lord instructed me in prayer not to call or write pastors asking for a place to minister. He told me to trust Him.

At the end of November 1989 I only had two scheduled places to minister. The first was a small church of a hundred people that met in a funeral home in South Carolina. This was booked for the first week of January. The other was scheduled for the end of February in a small church of two hundred members in Tennessee, and we were to be taken off the payroll the last week of December. We had to believe God.

Had I not learned to trust God for our finances while still an associate pastor, I would not have been able to handle the pressure when we were launched. It would have been too great an obstacle. I would have looked to man for my provision, instead of God. I most likely would have resorted to begging or scheming to raise the money we needed, and it would have consumed my efforts instead of seeking God for the messages He desired me to bring His people.

The low salary I received from my church ended up being a tremendous blessing. Had I listened to my friend who wanted to inform the senior pastor how to pay (honor) us, I don't know if we would be where we are today. Our first year of operating our ministry we had to believe God for one thousand dollars a week. At the time of this writing, we get to believe God for over one hundred thousand dollars a week to run the ministry.

If you are working for someone else, work with all your heart at the agreed salary. If you will honor your employer by doing a remarkable job, putting 100 percent of your effort forward, God will reward you in return. It'll come through either your employer or other avenues God chooses. Bottom line, you will be rewarded. When our church paid us a low salary, God honored us greatly; our house was filled with furniture, we drove a nice car, and we never lacked for food. We lived far above what we should have at the income we received. The scripture "A little that a righteous man has is better than the riches of many wicked" (Ps. 37:16) became very real to us. God was honoring us.

What's the conclusion? If you are an employee, establish this in your heart: if you honor God by giving 100 percent to your employer, you will receive a reward. On the other side of the spectrum, if you are an employer, know that you will benefit from the gifts blossoming in your employees by your honoring of them. Employers and pastors, you have a great reward from God hidden within your people; draw it out. Honor them in every way.

CHAPTER 14

Honor in the Home—Children

∽

After seven years of serving in a local church, and almost twenty years of traveling ministry, I've observed the greatest need for honor isn't in the church, or the workplace, but rather in our homes. The truth is, social, civil, and church arenas would all greatly benefit if fathers and mothers exemplified honor in their homes because it could not help but spill over to those who surround us.

The Power of a Parent's Word

In an earlier chapter we discussed the importance of children honoring their parents. The converse is also true. To honor is to value. If we value our children we'll treat and speak to them in such a way they will flourish in life.

Periodically I hear parents address their children in such demeaning ways I find myself cringing. It may be a father who speaks harshly to his tender daughter, or another who criticizes his son's skills on a playing field. It may be a mother who acts as though her children are an embarrassment, and in turn publicly humiliates them, the list goes on.

When my wife was in her teenage years, something developed that could have easily been averted. Lisa was an active teen and never overly obsessed with her weight. She was weighed at summer camp and physicals. Any weight increase was a function of normal growth.

Lisa swam nearly year round on two teams. This allowed her to eat practically whatever and whenever she wanted. Then there was an injury that caused her to sit out of swimming during her junior year of high school. Her activity level decreased, but she continued to consume the same amount of food as she had while training.

One day when she walked in from school, her father called her over. He looked Lisa up and down in a disapproving manner and then instructed her to turn around. Once his assessment was over he pronounced, "Boy, those jeans are tight! How much do you weigh?"

She volunteered her summer-camp weight.

He countered, "There's no way you weigh that! You're at least 135! Go weigh yourself!"

Feeling an overwhelming sense of shame and confusion, she proceeded to the family scale in her parents' bathroom. Lisa was surprised to discover she weighed close to 140 pounds.

Lisa reported back how much she weighed. Her father let her know in no uncertain terms how he felt it was far too much for her to weigh. It wasn't attractive, and guys were not going to ask her out at this weight. When the lecture was over, Lisa went back to her bedroom, undressed, and took a really good look at her body; for the first time she hated it. From that moment forward her weight became a driving force in her life. She became extremely self-conscious of her size, and consumed with thoughts about her weight. She ran and cut back on her food portions, and her efforts began to pay off. Boys began to notice her and she loved the attention. So eventually a parallel developed in her mind: *If I am thin, I am powerful and worthy of love and attention; and if I am fat, I am not.*

This mind-set put her into a downward spiral until she gradually deteriorated to a state of anorexia and bulimia. Lisa had a love-hate relationship with food. She loved to eat, but hated being fat. She turned to laxatives and diuretics to purge her body, and by her junior year in college her body became addicted to them. Eventually she was checked into the hospital because she had not had a bowel movement in over a month. At twenty-two years old God healed Lisa on every level, and her powerful testimony of this is found in her book *You Are Not What You Weigh*. But you do have to wonder, could much of this been avoided if her father handled Lisa's situation differently? What if he'd spoken words of affirmation and acceptance instead of degrading how she looked? What if he'd chosen a more constructive way to approach maintaining a healthy weight and food intake? Would Lisa's image of herself been different?

I have seen proof of how this works in our marriage. When I married Lisa she weighed 116 pounds. I made a point of constantly telling her she was beautiful and looked great in her outfits. I did not stop praising and affirming my wife after our first year of marriage or when she was pregnant or nursing. I just continued to say, "You are gorgeous," or "If you told me when I was twenty my wife would look this beautiful after so many years of marriage I would have had a party!" or "Wow, you're better looking today than the day I married you!" I've meant all these words, because that is how I see her. I believe this is my vantage because I'm constantly looking for ways to build Lisa up. As her husband this is one of my God-given responsibilities. Paul elaborates on this: "So husbands ought to love their own wives as their own bodies; he who loves his wife loves himself. For no one ever hated his own flesh, but *nourishes* and cherishes it, just as the Lord does the church" (Eph. 5:28–29, emphasis mine). Notice the word *nourish*; it means to give what is necessary for growth. I'm constantly looking for ways to nourish my wife with my words. This is something I'll cover more in-depth in the next chapter because it is all a part of honor.

While I was nourishing my wife, Lisa continued to believe the wisdom and promises God gave her when she was healed. God would continue to perfect those things that concerned her. By being supportive I created an atmosphere where my wife could believe God without hindrance. After twenty-five years of marriage and four children she still weighs what she did when we got married. She is not in the habit of working out, so some would say she is just genetically blessed. But I know better, because I remember the frightened, insecure girl who battled with her weight in her early twenties.

Children Are Rewards

Parents dishonor their children not only by harsh or negative words they speak, but also by neglecting to communicate praise or acceptance at the appropriate time. Children require frequent encouragement, direction, and affirmation. They need to be told, as well as shown, they are loved and valued. If not, chances are good they'll seek it in the wrong places. Sons and daughters seek approval, but if parents focus on immature traits or flaws they'll send the wrong message and reap the very opposite of what is needed for their children to grow and mature. Major damage can result when just a few words of affirmation could have made the adjustment, and the hurt would have been prevented. The irony of it all is these parents fail to see their roles in the outcome. Frustrated, they complain to friends about how difficult their children are; yet, more often than not the very traits they criticize could have been easily rectified through honor.

Words of a father and mother weigh so heavily in the life of a son or daughter. When defeat, failure, or weakness is spoken, the fallout in the child's life can range from a hindrance, all the way to serious issues. Often parents become increasingly discouraged with their child's behavior because it appears to be deteriorating, and a vicious cycle begins. If care is not taken this reactive treatment will distance the parents from the reward God bestows through our children. We read,

> "Behold, children are a heritage from the LORD, the fruit of the womb is a reward."
>
> —Ps. 127:3

We see in this scripture a direct reference of the reward promised through our children. Why don't more parents revel in this promise of the parent–child relationship? Rather, it seems to be just the opposite. Often I hear parents gripe about their young adults, "Oh, if I could only lock up my teenager until he or she reaches their twenties." Or, "Why can't we just bypass the teen years?" I remember hearing such statements when our four boys were still in their toddler years. It began to concern me; I thought to myself, *Are the boys going to turn into monsters in their young-adult years?*

However, I was granted some insight other parents don't often experience; so allow me to share these for your benefit. I served as a youth pastor when our oldest two were toddlers. In this position I was given a window into the homes of numerous families as I participated in pastoral counseling, and it wasn't long before I detected a pattern. I discovered that parents who focused their energies on criticizing their children's negative behavior found their children only growing worse. However, when parents spoke the promises of God over their children, these kids eventually grew into what was spoken. In light of Paul's second letter to the Corinthians this makes perfect sense: "While we do not look at the things which are seen, but at the things which are not seen. For the things which are seen are temporary, but the things which are not seen are eternal" (4:18).

The promises of God are found in the realm of the unseen truths outlined in His unchanging Word, which should be our focus. Lisa and I regularly speak God's promises over our children. Before they could talk we called them "disciples [taught by the Lord and obedient to His will], and great shall be the peace and undisturbed composure" (Isa. 54:13, AMP). And that they were our arrows (see Ps. 127:4), born for signs and wonders (see Isa. 8:18), and other such wonderful promises found in the Word of God.

We carefully chose their names by first investigating the root meanings and then praying for God's leading. We wanted to speak over them what they would become. Our firstborn Addison David's name carries the meaning "Beloved one worthy of trust." Our second-born Austin Michael's name means "Regal one who is like God." Our third, Joshua Alexander, carries the meaning "God saves and defends mankind." Our fourth is named Arden Christopher, which means "Ardent and fiery one who is Christlike." Each time we speak their names we are aware of what was being spoken over them. As their parents we have God-given privilege and authority to release blessing into their lives. Each son is growing into the characteristic of his name not because we merely confessed it, but because we believe what we spoke.

Did we have opportunities to believe they were the opposite of what we spoke? You would be naive to think we didn't. There were times they acted in ways completely opposite to their names. We had to bring correction and discipline, but we dealt with their behavior and protected what we spoke over their character. (As a side note, godly conflict is good, but when we attack character, rather than deal with behavior, our efforts become damaging.)

A Family Tragedy

I observed another life lesson as a youth pastor: the tragedy of not bringing needed discipline. Before discussing what I personally witnessed, let me first exemplify this from Scripture.

King David had many sons by different wives. We'll focus on two: his oldest, Amnon, and his third born, Absalom. Amnon did a very wicked thing to his half sister Tamar, Absalom's full sister. He pretended to be ill and asked his father to send Tamar to serve him food. When she came in he sent the servants out and raped her. He then despised the very sight of her and threw her out of his chamber. He had disgraced a royal virgin princess, and devastated her life with shame.

Her brother Absalom was outraged by the wickedness of Amnon. He hated his half brother for defiling his sister. He waited silently; surely King David would execute discipline and justice on Amnon.

Time passed and nothing was done though the king; though he was displeased, he took no action. Absalom was devastated. He brought his sister Tamar into his home and provided for her.

She once wore the royal robes reserved for virgin daughters of the king; now she was robed in shame. A beautiful young girl once highly esteemed by her people lived a life of seclusion. Who would want to marry her when she was no longer a virgin? It was so unfair. Her life was over, while the man who committed this atrocity went about his life as if nothing happened. She bore the weight of it all as she wandered through a life in shambles.

Day after day Absalom saw his grieving sister. The dream of a princess was now a nightmare. Absalom waited a year and still his father did nothing. Alongside his hatred of Amnon a resentment of his father took root in Absalom's heart as well.

Two years passed and his hatred for Amnon turned to thoughts of murder as Absalom carefully plotted how he would avenge his sister. Why shouldn't he when those who had the proper authority chose to do nothing? Absalom held a banquet for all David's sons, and when Amnon least expected it Absalom killed him and fled to Geshur. His vengeance against Amnon was satisfied. However, the dark offense he harbored toward his father for not taking action burned stronger while in exile. To add fuel to the fire he stewed over the question, *Why hasn't my father sent for me?* This offense eventually turned to hatred.

As Absalom's thoughts became further poisoned with bitterness he became an expert in David's weaknesses. A critical veneer shrouded his life. Yet he still hoped his father would call for him. David did not. This fueled his hatred. Imagine his thoughts: *My father is so hailed by the people, but they are blind to his true nature. He is a self-seeking man who merely uses God as a cover-up. Why, he is worse than his predecessor Saul! He lost his throne for refusing to kill the king of the Amalekites and sparing a few of their best sheep and oxen. My father committed adultery with the wife of one of his most loyal men. Then covered his sin by killing the very man who was loyal to him. He is a murderer; he is an adulterer, that is why he did not punish Amnon!*

Absalom spent three years in Geshur. David was over the death of his son Amnon, and Joab convinced the king to bring Absalom back to Jerusalem.

Time passed. Absalom's hatred grew and he began to draw to him those who were likewise discontent with his father. He accomplished this by making himself available to all Israel. He listened to their complaints; all the while lamenting the fact that if only he were king he could help them, but alas he was not. He judged the cases the king had no time for. Perhaps Absalom judged these cases because he had not been served justice in his own life. He gave the appearance of genuine concern for the people. The Bible says Absalom stole the hearts of Israel from his father David. But did he truly care for them or was he seeking a way to overthrow his father, whom he now hated?

Absalom drew Israel to himself and rose up against his father. The conflict became so intense King David had to flee for his life. For a while, it looked as though Absalom would establish himself as the new king, but the tables were turned when he was killed in his pursuit of David. This judgment happened even though David ordered that his son remain untouched.

Absalom was consumed by his own hatred and bitterness. He was the one with so much potential, an heir to the throne who died in his prime. Could this have been avoided by his father bringing correction to Amnon? It's quite possible. How about Tamar? She most likely ended up bitter and alone. Would her life have been different had her father punished Amnon? Certainly. I believe these tragedies could all have been avoided had David honored his children by bringing godly discipline. David dishonored all his children by refusing to bring correction to the one.

Dishonor by Withholding Discipline

Let's return to what I observed as a youth pastor. Many parents who sat in my office because they were having problems with their children didn't believe in discipline. Like King David, they simply refused to chasten their children. They believed in "loving" their sons and daughters out of their disobedient behavior, but their approach wasn't working. Their children were in terrible shape; they were both rebellious and disrespectful, and their attitude bled over into every area involving authority figures . . . school, work, youth group, and so forth.

Interestingly, the response of these young people who were "loved" rather than disciplined was to despise their parents. It was both ironic and tragic. Ironic, because the very thing the parents were trying to do—win their children's love—was lost as the very opposite response occurred. Tragic, because these children made damaging decisions that would prove costly to their families for years to come.

I recall sharply correcting one young woman for how she spoke to her parents as they were all gathered in my office. I thought, *Why am I doing this? Why didn't her mother or father correct her?* They were committed to their course of trying to "love" their children out of evil behavior when in reality the Word of God tells us parents who do not discipline their children actually hate them:

> "He who spares his rod hates his son, but he who loves him disciplines him promptly."
>
> —Prov. 13:24

I watched these young people grow up with messed-up lives. They ran into many hard times and trouble, which could have been avoided had they received proper training early in life. Why? Because, "The rod and rebuke give wisdom, but a child left to himself brings shame to his mother" (Prov. 29:15). Why didn't these parents listen to the counsel of God's Word? They thought they were wiser and in essence they dishonored both God and their children.

The pattern was consistent: when parents failed to correct their children, their children ended up despising them. On the other hand, when parents were overly harsh and dishonoring of their children, their children resented their parents. They were often wounded in their soul, which caused them personality dysfunctions. Many wrestled with fear issues.

When our children misbehaved, we found discipline was most successful when it was swift and concise. Afterward it was over. It is unhealthy to carry grudges or resentment. In a short matter of time there would be laughter and hugs all around. When they are forgiven it is like it didn't happen. When God forgives us, He remembers our sin no more. Discipline is assurance they will learn from their mistakes, yet not carry guilt.

Lisa particularly honored our children by way of nurture, love, and affection. I was the stronger advocate of consistent godly discipline. We learned to draw on each other's strengths. Through Lisa's example, I learned to be more verbally and physically affectionate, and through my example, Lisa gleaned the value of discipline. As a result of joining the strengths God gave each of us, we've seen His blessing surround the lives of our children.

An Earlier than Expected Reward

Our oldest son Addison graduated with high honors from high school and was accepted in one of the top ten business universities in the nation. He was scheduled to begin classes in September 2005.

As a summer job, Addison worked for our ministry in previous years, and he was doing the same before he began university. In early July I received a call from him. His voice was a bit nervous as he asked, "Dad, can I talk to you about something?"

I could immediately tell it was a serious issue and prepared myself. I replied, "Sure, what would you like to discuss?"

He said, "Dad, do I have to go to university this September? I want to continue to work at the ministry full time. I want to help you and Mom get this message out."

It didn't take long for me to reply. I knew he had a strong walk with God and wouldn't have approached me about this unless he'd prayed about it. In my heart it seemed right, and I was thrilled and honored. I replied, "That would be great, we'd love to having you as a full-time staff member."

Now let me tell you what transpired over the next year and a half. After only a few months of Addison working for us, I was approached by our director of staff who recommended Addison for the position of supervisor over Church Relations. This department has been in existence for several years and works with the churches and pastors to supply them with the DVD curricula and workbooks which accompany many of our books. At the time of this writing, there are approximately fourteen thousand churches in the USA and over one thousand churches in Australia who use them.

The recommendation of the promotion didn't come because Addison is our son. I specifically requested that our children receive no special treatment. Actually I think it was often harder for them because they have to navigate both the family and employee dynamics. My staff overseer complied with this request, so I knew when he asked me this, it was solely based on my son's job performance and leadership skills.

I agreed to his recommendation, and I am still astounded by the results. Over the next year our church relationship department tripled their growth. Everywhere I traveled I was greeted with stories of how pastors developed relationships with the great group of guys working in Addison's department. Addison has a gift for motivating, and his enthusiasm is contagious. Pastors were prayed for, questions were answered, and requests were serviced in a timely manner through his leadership.

I discovered by honoring my son, God rewarded not only me but our entire organization through him. Jesus told us that if we honored one of the little ones we would by no means lose our reward. My oldest son lifted a weight off us and expanded our relationships in way I could never have imagined. He has actually been the source of some amazing Kingdom connections. Who would have thought a twenty-year-old had so much in him? Not only that, but many churches I may never be able to visit have received the Word of God through the curriculum resources. This ultimately means more lives are impacted for eternity!

I stand in awe of my sons. For years I've prayed, "Father, these boys are not my boys, they are Your boys; I'm only a steward of those who belong to You. So Lord, You may do whatever You desire with them. If You want them on the other side of the planet, may Your will be done. I just ask that they would fulfill Your will for their lives."

I really mean what I've prayed. I know there is a good chance distance may one day separate us, however, thus far, God has given us the privilege of working closely with our son. Now our other sons are already talking about coming on board soon. In one sense, we've already received a glimpse of the reward of honoring our children. Though this happens on multiple levels and seasons, it is already apparent.

I see this same pattern with other parents who honor their sons and daughters. If children are valued they will flourish, and in their flourishing God has certain rewards to give to those who've honored them. Those rewards make us more productive in touching lives eternally. It is His Word, it is His plan, it is a spiritual law spoken by the lips of Jesus Himself. When parents discipline well, love well, and thus honor their children well in obedience to God, we are promised a godly return. There will be joy in our latter years rather than sorrow. Strength and support will surround our golden years with promise.

CHAPTER 15

Honor in the Home—Wife

∞

I t's not only the children in households under authority but also the wife. We spoke in an earlier chapter of the importance of the wife honoring her husband. Again, as with the children, the flip side is true.

Honor Your Wife

Peter says,

> "Husbands, likewise, dwell with them with understanding, giving honor to the wife, as to the weaker vessel."
>
> —1 Pet. 3:7

Peter specifically states wives are to be given honor. Some men interpret this verse as the wife being beneath her husband in spiritual things. No, "weaker vessel" doesn't mean your wife is below you; it only means she can't bench-press as much as you. The physical strength of the average woman is less than the average man. The Amplified Bible records this verse "honoring the woman as [physically] weaker." Hear Peter's words in the New Living Translation: "In the same way, you husbands must give honor to your wives. Treat her with understanding as you live together. She may be weaker than you are, but she is your equal partner in God's gift of new life. If you don't treat her as you should, *your prayers will not be heard*" (emphasis mine).

We are equal partners—joint heirs—of the inheritance of grace. However, in the final part of this verse we see a startling and remarkable statement having to do with answered prayer: if a husband dishonors his wife, his prayers will not be heard. Wow, that's sobering! This is a miserable life for anyone. Just think about it, the throne room will not listen to your prayers, your words will not even reach the ears of God, if you dishonor your wife. That's enough to grab my complete attention. It calls for considerable pondering on our part as husbands. The good news is the converse is also true; if you honor your wife you will have confidence in prayer before God.

Let me take a moment and speak directly to you husbands. Do you treat your wife as valuable? Do you listen to her words, or do you shun her, thinking to yourself, *Oh, she's just an emotional female?* I've learned my lesson in this the hard way. I belittled the counsel of my wife when we were first married. However, over time I noticed repeatedly she would say things that eventually proved to be the wisdom of God. I saw myself as the more spiritual one; oh, how very wrong I was.

After Lisa was accurate on several occasions concerning various topics, I took this matter to prayer. I protested, "God, I pray sometimes two hours a day, she prays maybe ten or twenty minutes, and many times those prayers are in the shower." (I was wrong about this as well; my wife lives a life of prayer, communing on a regular basis in everyday life with God—something I learned how to do later.)

I continued, "Why is she right so often on important matters and I'm wrong?"

The Lord's reply was immediate. "Son, draw a circle on a piece of paper."

I did.

"Now put X-marks all over the inside of the circle."

I did that as well.

He continued. "Now draw a line right down the middle of the circle [thus creating two halves]. You'll notice roughly 50 percent of the X-marks are on one half the circle, and the rest are on the other half."

I acknowledged.

The Lord then said, "The X-marks represent My wisdom and counsel; the information you need to make wise decisions. The circle is one, but it is divided into two halves. You're one half and Lisa is the other. You are one flesh, representing the complete circle, even though you are still individuals, represented by each half of the circle. But the circle is not complete if you only look at your half."

He continued. "You will notice half of the wisdom and counsel is located on Lisa's side and the other half is on your side. You've been making all your family decisions based off half the information needed from Me, just your side. You've not been drawing on My information from her side. I'll give you needed information, and her needed information, but as a wise leader you must learn to draw out from Lisa what I show her, and discuss the matter together before making the final decision as the leader of the home."

That one encounter with God totally changed my married life. I then realized when I was a single man, I was a full circle; and now as a married man, being one flesh with my wife, I could no longer live the way I did when single.

The Weaker Vessel

Look again at Peter's words: "Husbands, likewise, dwell with them with understanding, giving honor to the wife, as to the weaker vessel, and as being heirs together in the grace of life, that your prayers may not be hindered." We are to dwell with our wives with understanding. God's word to me in prayer, which I've just shared, gave me needed understanding to dwell successfully with my wife.

There is so much more understanding to be gained from the Word of God on how to dwell successfully in marriage with your wife. Many divorces could be averted if men only took the time to seek the wisdom of how women differ from men. You take the masculine and the feminine and put the two together and you'll find the complete reflection of the image of God. Oh yes, you cannot see God's nature in just the male, or just the female. How do we know this? Scripture tells us, "So God created man (*mankind or human beings*) in His own image; in the image of God He created him, male and female He created them" (Gen. 1:27, words in parentheses mine).

God created "him" in His own image, but "him" is spelled out "male and female." Scripture specifically mentions it takes the male and the female to give us the representation of mankind, and mankind is created in the image of God. For this reason Paul states, "Nevertheless, neither is man independent of woman, nor woman independent of man, in the Lord" (1 Cor. 11:11).

Returning to Peter's words we hear him say that the man is to honor his wife in two ways: first as the weaker vessel, and second as a joint heir in the grace of life. Let's briefly discuss the first. We are to honor our wives as weaker vessels. This means we treat them like ladies. Men are strong, and we are to use our strength to protect our wives. This instruction would also apply to the simple things as well, such as opening doors for her, pulling out the chair in the restaurant before she's seated, protecting her from rude people, and so forth.

Since the husband is the head of the home, we should prefer our wives. That means if you only have enough money to buy one new outfit for a special occasion, show you value her by insisting to buy a new outfit for her, rather than yourself. When choosing a vacation spot, if she wants to go to one location and you another, go with her choice. To lead in the Kingdom is to serve, not to dominate. As husband, the only time your decisions should override your wife's desire is when you're certain it's the best option for her, the family, or the kingdom of God. Otherwise, always prefer her desires to yours. This is one reason you are made leader over her, to lay down your life for her. This is honoring your wife and you will be blessed and rewarded, and your prayers will not be hindered.

Joint Heir

According to Peter, the other specific reason we are to honor our wives is that they are joint heirs in the grace of life. This means she is equal in her standing with God. You don't have an advantage with God because you are a man. Some believe this lie of male superiority deep in their hearts, and it's ludicrous. This canard was conceived by chauvinistic men who will one day stand before the throne of God and give an account. It's become obvious to me in almost twenty years of traveling ministry, along with studying the Scripture, the favor of God is withheld from families or churches that view women as being spiritually inferior to men. In fact, you'll find spiritual oppression, heaviness, and bondage in these places.

We need to ask ourselves some questions. In some churches, why are women not included in the leadership teams? Why are females not allowed to minister on Sunday mornings? Why are women not included on the pastoral teams of certain churches? Why in leadership do we only have the fathers' voices, rather than the mothers' voices? A church without a mother's voice is no different than a family without a mother, only a father to raise the children. It can be done, but a very significant influence is missing, and the children suffer. In families where mothers have tragically died or possibly left, God gives grace to the man to raise healthy children. However, when churches shun the voices of mothers the grace is lacking, for the church has shunned the wisdom of God.

You may protest, "But the Bible says a leader has to be the husband of one wife." Let's address what Paul writes: "A church leader must be without fault; he must have only one wife" (1 Tim. 3:2, TEV).

This statement is indeed gender specific, not gender neutral; a leader must have only one wife. However, we must think through what's being said in the light of all Scripture. Paul is writing to people who were accustomed to reading the Old Testament Scriptures. In the Old Testament you'll find many cases of men having more than one wife: Abraham, King David, Solomon, Jacob, Elkanah (the husband of Hannah and Peninnah), and that's just to name a few. However, you'll not find one incident in the Old Testament of a woman having more than one husband. It was not customary, nor even allowed, as it was contrary to the law. So why would Paul have to write that a woman must only have one husband in order to be a church leader? It wouldn't be necessary. You may think I'm stretching it; however, if we are to so strictly adhere to the letter of his words, then we would have to eliminate single men from leadership positions in the church, because they are not the husband of one wife either. If that were the case, Paul would have eliminated himself from being a leader in the church, which is ridiculous. Some of us have been very narrow-minded in this area.

It is not about gender; it is about the call and gift of God on a person's life. Men who have discouraged their wives, or the women in their church, from ministering in their callings have to a large degree shut up the window of heaven over their homes and ministries. Yes, there can be areas of blessing, but the full blessing of heaven will be missing.

The body of Christ has been crippled due to the dishonor shown toward women. However, the good news is this: it will not stay this way. For the prophet Joel and the apostle Peter both foretold by the Spirit of God the full restoration of women in ministry in the final days of the church. These men stated, "This is what I will do in the last days, God says: I will pour out my Spirit on everyone. Your sons and daughters will proclaim my message; your young men will see visions, and your old men will have dreams. Yes, even on my servants, both men and women, I will pour out my Spirit in those days, and they will proclaim my message" (Acts 2:17–18, TEV). Notice both men and women will proclaim the Word of God. This is also foretold by the psalmist: "The Lord gave the word; great was the company of those who proclaimed it" (Ps. 68:11). Who specifically are those who proclaim the Word of God? You have to go to other translations to find the answer: "The Lord gives the word [of power]; the women who bear and publish [the news] are a great host" (Ps. 68:11, AMP).

It's not men and women the psalmist focuses on, but specifically the women. Let me share with you other translations: "The Lord gave the command, and many women carried the news" (TEV); and again, "The Lord announces victory, and throngs of women shout the happy news" (NLT). Women are to proclaim the Word of God, and not just to other ladies, but to men as well. We see this truth confirmed with Jesus. Isn't it interesting that the first evangelist was Mary Magdalene? Jesus Himself was the One who commissioned her. We read: "Jesus said to her, 'Do not cling to Me, for I have not yet ascended to My Father; but go to My brethren and say to them, "I am ascending to My Father and your Father, and to My God and your God.'" Mary Magdalene came and told the disciples that she had seen the Lord, and that He had spoken these things to her" (John 20:17–18).

Let's take this further. If you go to the Gospel of Luke you'll find that Mary was the lead speaker. Jesus sent not only her but a group of women to proclaim the Lord's resurrection to the apostles. We read, "It was Mary Magdalene, Joanna, Mary the mother of James, and the other women with them, who told these things to the apostles" (24:10). So women proclaimed the Word of God to men, and Jesus was the One who sent them!

Isn't it interesting that the first to speak to others, both men and women, in the temple of the Messiah's arrival was Anna the prophetess? Simeon was the first to speak to Joseph and Mary, however the first to speak to multitudes in the temple was Anna. We read, "And coming in that instant she gave thanks to the Lord, and spoke of Him to all those who looked for redemption in Jerusalem" (Luke 2:38).

Isn't it interesting Philip had four daughters who spoke the word of the Lord? We read, "He had four unmarried daughters who proclaimed God's message" (Acts 21:9, TEV). They proclaimed under divine inspiration the word of the Lord. How can we fulfill the Great Commission if over half the body of Christ is not honored to fulfill their calling? When men nurture the call of God in their wives' lives they will receive a great reward. I've seen this in my own life.

(*Note: there are a couple scriptures in the New Testament that on the surface would appear to contradict what I've written. Again, these scriptures need to be studied to know the intent of what was written, and the purpose of this book is not to delve into this subject. However, there are excellent resources available by respected leaders who've studied these verses thoroughly, one of which is *Why Not Women* by Loren Cunningham and David Joel Hamilton.)

My Wife

Lisa had an eye removed when she was five years old. She had a disease called retinal blastoma, which, simply put, is cancer of the retina. All through school, and to this day, she wears a prosthesis in her right eye socket. As you probably can imagine, she was ridiculed and made fun of in school. Some of the names ascribed to her by immature classmates were Cyclops and One-Eye. There were times she ran home during the middle of the day crying. Her mother wisely encouraged her to remain strong and ignore bullies; but it still stung.

In high school, Lisa discovered two classes required to graduate that terrified and challenged her above all others. One was speech; the other was typing. After attempting both without success, she met with her guidance counselor pleading to be exempted from these required classes. How could she stand in front of people and effectively communicate? Typing was nearly impossible because she lost all sense of spatial awareness. The counselor compassionately agreed and excused Lisa from the two courses; other classes were added in to take their place.

As stated in an earlier chapter, Lisa came to know Jesus Christ at the close of her college years. We were soon thereafter married and moved to Dallas, Texas, and attended a large church. At the time she was more reserved and not at all outgoing. The women of the church perceived her mannerisms as haughty and stuck up. But the reality was vastly different from the signals she sent. She still carried many of the fears developed from having an eye removed, and the ridicule that followed throughout her school years.

Early in our marriage we needed two incomes, so Lisa signed up with a direct-marketing makeup and skin care firm. I attended some of her classes and discovered that my wife was gifted in this area and had a good working knowledge of the products. But Lisa was intimidated. She was afraid to tell anyone about the products, so I had to initiate contacts and presentations for her.

A year later, as we walked through a major upscale department store in Dallas, I commented, "Lisa, you need to apply for a position in cosmetics. You are better than all these ladies who sell and apply makeup."

She argued that I was wrong, but she was scheduled to work in the mall that week at another store, and every time she walked thru the doors my words echoed in her ears. So in secret she went and applied, and to her surprise ended up getting the job!

She was hired as a representative for Elizabeth Arden. The girl who previously sold the line struggled. Lisa came on and sold almost completely out of stock in a few short weeks. One day she turned to the sound of a briefcase slamming down on her counter; it was an executive of the company. He said, "We're going to lunch, Lisa, you are not staying here any longer!"

She interviewed at his request and was promoted to account co-ordinator, which meant she oversaw sixteen stores in the Dallas and Fort Worth area, and one in New Mexico and another in Oklahoma. In less than two years she was again promoted to promotional repre-sentative of the company and given an eight-state territory. She re-ceived a large salary increase along with some major benefits, which included a brand-new company car, a Ford Thunderbird. Guess who got to ride along in the car, and sometimes drive it? And who also benefited from her salary increase? I did. It's called honor's reward!

A couple years later we moved to Florida where I took a youth pastor's position in a very large church. After several months I told our young people Lisa would be ministering to them in my stead the following week. I could see the Lord had placed so much in Lisa, and she could communicate and teach well at home. I knew she could do the same before a group of people. Needless to say my an-nouncement met with considerable resistance—not with the young people, but from Lisa. She protested for the entire week, "You can't make me do this! I can't speak to the youth. I have nothing to say." I just assured her she did and God would help her do it. I saw the gift in her and didn't want it left dormant.

She spoke a week later and did an amazing job. The young peo-ple were so excited to hear from Lisa. I did it a few more times in the ensuing months. Each occasion was met with the same resistance. Each time she argued, "I've already preached everything I know to them."

I laughed and said, "I do that every week, and I have to depend on God each new week." It didn't seem to comfort her very much.

However, each time she spoke, it just kept getting richer and richer. The young people loved her.

After being released from staff by our pastor and launched into the ministry we now have, I began to do the same thing. While in communities speaking at small conferences, I would announce periodically, without consulting Lisa, that she would take the next session. The first time I did this, Lisa was so upset she kept me up half the night. "I can't believe you volunteered me to take your session. This isn't your youth group, but an out-of-town conference. I'm not doing it, you are."

Then she asked what I shared in my session because she had stayed in the room and put our kids to bed. When I told her, she freaked. "You preached my only message at your service tonight, so what am I suppose to speak on tomorrow morning?"

I simply said, "Honey, there is so much God has taught you, and these people need to hear it."

She continued arguing until three o'clock in the morning. Finally, I just started laughing and said, "Honey, you're speaking at nine a.m., that is only six hours away, you better get some sleep."

Sure enough, the next morning Lisa hit it out of the park. Her message was amazing and the people received so wonderfully. I continued to do this in various cities, and she kept ministering more powerfully.

Now let me say something. This doesn't mean it was easy for her. The first time she spoke to a mixed audience of college- and career-aged kids, a small percentage of the men present stood up noisily and walked out refusing to listen to a woman to teach. Understand at that moment Lisa wanted to join them. She has never sought to put herself in front of others. She did out of obedience to God.

The Same with Writing

I did the same thing with writing. I'd written three books and Lisa helped with the editing process. I recognized she was a gifted writer, and my third book, *The Bait of Satan*, became a national bestseller. I approached the publisher and commented, "My wife has a message of how God has delivered her from fear and control in certain areas of her life. You should talk to Lisa about a book, but don't do it through me, go directly to her."

A few weeks later, the publisher came to our home. But unbeknownst to Lisa, he wasn't visiting me; he came for her. She looked at me as if to say, "What is going on here?"

He set up a meeting so their staff could listen to her share what was on her heart. After a while he stated, "Your husband believes you carry a very important message that needs to be in writing. Now after listening to you, I feel the same way."

As of this date Lisa has written six books, five of which have been bestsellers. Through the influence of her books she has touched lives all over the world. She now stands before tens of thousands of people each year, and co-hosts our television program, which reaches over two hundred nations.

Think of it, here is a woman who opted out of speech and typing. What does she now do on a regular basis? Speaks to thousands on platforms, through television, and other venues; and she types books! And how does she do it? She faced her fear through the power of God's grace. Because of the prompting of her husband, who recognized and honored God's gift in His daughter, many lives have been blessed. So what would happen if all the husbands in the church began to honor their wives?

What has been my reward for honoring my wife? There have been so many it would be impossible to record them all. Lisa's life has flourished on every level and not just in ministry. When someone gets free, they are free indeed. Just as I thought God's grace opened doors for Lisa, now her gift has done the same for me. Many significant doors have been opened to me all over the world because of Lisa. I've been invited to a number of places where the leaders stated, "Your wife touched the lives of our women so deeply we had to also invite you."

Another reward is the fact that I live with a fulfilled woman. When someone is not living in the call of God on their life, they are heavy in heart, because they are not giving expression to what God created them to do. They are weighed down. However, when you are in the will of God, Jesus says His burden is light (see Matt. 11:28–30). There is joy in laboring for Him; even though the attacks are heavier and more frequent, it's easier in the plan of God. My wife has been so much happier and enthusiastic as a daughter of God, wife, mother, and minister of the gospel. If one of those elements were missing, the other areas would suffer. She's been careful to keep her priorities right; our family comes before the work of the ministry, and there has been an amazing grace on the family to release her to travel and fulfill her call. Our marriage has never been so full, or our love so strong as it is in obeying God's call on our lives.

Another reward, which I believe is the greatest, is hundreds of thousands of lives being impacted for eternity as a result of Lisa's ministering the Word of God. One day we'll be privileged to see the magnitude of the far-reaching effects of her labor at the throne of God. I asked my sons one day, "Boys, do you see your mom and dad's frequent travel to minister as a negative thing? Do you see it as us being taken from you, or do you see it positively, as your part in the ministry—sowing your mom and dad into the lives of needy people all over the world?"

My oldest was the first to speak up: "Dad, we see it as our part in the ministry. It's our way of touching people's lives for the Kingdom." The other three boys strongly agreed.

At that moment Lisa and I looked at each other with such joy. We realized how great the grace of God is upon His servants to simply obey Him. Our boys will receive a great reward, not only in this life but also at the judgment seat of Christ. How amazing to see the reward of honor. We didn't see it at first, but it's overtaken us just as the Word of God promises: "Now it shall come to pass, if you diligently obey the voice of the LORD your God, to observe carefully all His commandments which I command you today, that . . . all these blessings shall come upon you and overtake you, because you obey the voice of the LORD your God" (Deut. 28:1–2).

We don't honor just to get a reward; we honor because it is the heart of God, and it is our delight. However, the reward is surer than the seed bringing forth its fruit. Rewards follow all true honor. So husbands, don't delay. Honor your wife as a way of life; the reward God has to give to you through her is more than you can imagine.

CHAPTER 16

Honor All

∽

Let's briefly discuss honoring those outside the home, church, or office. In short, they are those we come in contact with in everyday life. Peter simply says:

"Honor all people."

—1 Pet. 2:17

It couldn't be any plainer. Let's look at some other translations: "Show respect for all men [treat them honorably]" (AMP), and "Treat everyone you meet with dignity" (The Message), and again, "Show respect for everyone" (NLT). These are the ones Jesus affectionately ascribed to as our "neighbor." You've probably heard the famous story; let's read it from The Message:

"There was once a man traveling from Jerusalem to Jericho. On the way he was attacked by robbers. They took his clothes, beat him up, and went off leaving him half-dead. Luckily, a priest was on his way down the same road, but when he saw him he angled across to the other side. Then a

Levite religious man showed up; he also avoided the injured man.

"A Samaritan traveling the road came on him. When he saw the man's condition, his heart went out to him. He gave him first aid, disinfecting and bandaging his wounds. Then he lifted him onto his donkey, led him to an inn, and made him comfortable. In the morning he took out two silver coins and gave them to the innkeeper, saying, 'Take good care of him. If it costs any more, put it on my bill—I'll pay you on my way back.'

"What do you think? Which of the three became a neighbor to the man attacked by robbers?"

"The one who treated him kindly," the religion scholar responded.

Jesus said, "Go and do the same."

—Luke 10:30–38

The priest and the Levite didn't view the man close to death as valuable. The Samaritan, who was a foreigner, did. Scripture specifically states, "His heart went out to him"; again, all true honor originates from the heart. He took the time to give the wounded man what was needed to live, and even went beyond the necessities, by putting him up in an inn. In fact, he gave two days' wages to care for one he'd never met before. He didn't need to hear a word from God, nor did he have to pray about it. Out of a heart of love, compassion, and respect for other individuals, he did what was necessary. This is a classic example of honoring all men.

Modern-Day Examples

One of the great modern-day stories exemplifying this occurred with my friend Bill Wilson. Bill's mother left him sitting on a culvert when he was a young boy of eleven. She told him to stay put until she returned. She never did. A Christian man found him and paid for Bill to attend a summer camp. That unselfish act by this man set something in motion.

Years later Bill Wilson founded, and today leads, Metro Ministries, which reaches out to over twenty thousand children in New York City every week. He still drives a bus, and along with his staff and volunteers, they reach out to neighborhoods in great need to teach the gospel, both in deed and word. It's an amazing ministry; one that has saved thousands of lives not only in New York City but in other places as well. Bill has inspired people nationally and internationally to value helpless children, and established numerous Metro Ministries around the world.

There are many, like Bill, who reach out to underprivileged or helpless people. We can assist them. How? One of the best ways is supporting their outreaches through prayer or money. Can you imagine what would happen if every person who professes Christianity gave something every month to a ministry like this? Can you imagine how many would come into the Kingdom? Imagine the man injured in Jesus' parable as the sinner and the Samaritan a true believer. After being cared for, he would have gladly listened to the gospel the Samaritan preached. However, if the Levite or the priest had been the Christian, the wounded man wouldn't want much to do with their gospel. When God's love burns in our hearts, we will value all men and join financially with ministries like these that help the desperately needy, coupled with proclaiming the good news of the gospel to them.

Another way of helping is by joining their teams. You don't have to move to Brooklyn, New York, or another distant city where ministries like Bill's are based; get involved with one of your local church outreaches. Even if it's one day a month, you'll be touching lives on an organized level to reach people in need. Together we can do so much more than we can alone, although this is not meant to take away from the individual effort exemplified by the Samaritan. However, Scripture emphasizes how much more we can accomplish by cooperating with others: "Five of you shall chase a hundred, and a hundred of you shall put ten thousand to flight" (Lev. 26:8, AMP). Our effectiveness increases when we join together. We must remember, God has ordained the church in such a way that we need each other for effectiveness. Paul states that the body of Christ will grow when all the members work together (see Eph. 4:16). This is another important reason to be planted in the local organized church. Bottomline, if every believer did his or her part, both individually and through structured ministries, how many more Bill Wilson stories would we have?

As important as Bill's outreach is, we can't stop here. There are also countless multitudes who aren't impoverished; who do possess the necessities or even luxuries of life, but are hurting, or even destitute, in their souls. Some of these are found in wealthy neighborhoods, not just the run-down "hoods"; in short, they are everywhere. You meet them at the grocery store, at the mall, at work. They are lonely or hurting humanity, and they need to be valued. They, too, are our neighbors.

We come across these people every day. Sometimes due to being focused on our own business we're undiscerning of their needs. The older I've grown, the more I've come to realize how easy it is to reach out to these people. It all begins with simply receiving in our hearts the charge to honor all people. If we do this, we become sensitive and are led, many times unconsciously, by the Spirit of God, and everyday life becomes continuous ministry. When you honor people, you will not ignore or speak rudely to those God brings across your path; rather you walk in a divine flow that brings the living waters of heaven to the thirsty in heart. A scripture I love and have cleaved to for years in regard to these people is, "The LORD God has given Me the tongue of the learned, that I should know how to speak a word in season to him who is weary. He awakens me morning by morning, He awakens My ear to hear as the learned" (Isa. 50:4).

You can believe God for this promise. Many will not speak to people out of fear they may say something stupid. If you simply believe God's word in this scripture, you can confidently know your words will bring life, healing, and strength to those who are weary and destitute in their souls.

But we're still not finished, because it goes even further. The term "all men" reaches beyond the destitute. Everyone we come in contact with will flourish if we honor him or her. Every kind word spoken from our hearts will minister life to the hearers. Essentially, it includes the myriads of people we come in contact with on a daily basis, many of which, we'll only see once. It could be the person we meet on the elevator, or the flight attendant, or the operator we speak to on the phone. We can honor them with a warm greeting or just through a sincere smile.

Recently, while I was walking in a park in London, an old middle-eastern woman was coming my way with her head down. I was moved with compassion toward her. I imagined she wasn't accustomed to being treated as valuable, especially by a man. My heart went out to her, so I purposefully said a hearty and cheerful good morning. Her eyes looked up at me almost in disbelief. I could almost hear her thoughts: *Why would a Western man speak with such kindness to a stranger, and a woman at that?* But before she could dwell on those issues, her desire to be valued took over, and her entire countenance changed; she timidly returned a greeting. I most likely will not see her again in this life, but I believe the love of God that reached out from my heart sowed an eternal seed in her that will one day produce fruit. We can have faith for this; let's live in the Spirit and believe we don't just exist, but are ambassadors who live in the supernatural power of God to bring life to people.

Is it hard to smile at people? Is it so difficult to say kind words to strangers? Is it too hard to believe our every word will minister life? It is, if you lack faith in the power of God and honor is lacking in your heart for all people. But if you will pray and ask God to put genuine honor in your heart for those He died for, He'll do it, because it's His desire.

A Way of Life

Once you've asked God to put honor in your heart for all people, your whole life will change. You'll treat the waiter or waitress much differently. You'll not just stare at the menu and issue your order for food; you'll look them in the eyes and greet them when they first approach your table. You'll ask the server what his or her name is before you order, and each time you address them call them by name; and most important you'll verbally and financially thank them for serving you that meal. Don't leave a 10 percent tip; if you value them you'll leave a 20, maybe even 25 percent tip. Always do more than the standard. Don't settle for average. Ask yourself how valuable the waiter is. The answer is one you should be well aware of—precious enough for Jesus to die for.

I'm sad to report there have been a few occasions when ministers took me out to eat, and I've had to observe the miserly tip they left the one who served us. In one of those incidents, the tip was so awful I just had to do something. The pastor and I were walking out to the parking lot and I simply said, "Go ahead and get your car, I need to run back into the restaurant." While he got his vehicle I returned to leave a larger tip on the table. How could the one who served us be treated in such a menial manner, especially since the waiter knew we had just come from a service?

I recall one time; Lisa and I left a 50 percent tip for the one who served us a meal. She knew we were in the ministry from our con-versations. We were God's link to her, and she needed to know He valued her. We left before she discovered how much we gave, but I'm confident she was touched, and a good flavor of the Savior was left in her. Paul says, "For we are to God the fragrance of Christ among those who are being saved and among those who are perishing" (2 Cor. 2:15). Her view of ministry is most likely now on a positive note, and that will keep her open to receive from another in the future.

When you honor those who serve you, many times you'll receive favorable treatment—larger portions, extra food, better service, or other surprises. Believers shouldn't honor for this reason, but nevertheless, it is a blessing. Lisa and I many times use the valet parking at the airport. Because we travel so much they've come to recognize our car. If there are a few people on the job, they'll almost race out to our vehicle so they can be the first to serve us. Why? Because we give them good tips. We also talk to them and ask how things are going for them and their loved ones. At our airport there is valet parking under cover, protected from the weather, and other spaces that are in the open, vulnerable to the weather. My car is always put under cover. It's called honor's reward.

In our local grocery store it's the same way. There have been out-of-town guests who have gone into the store with Lisa and me, and they've commented, "Who doesn't know you in this store?" It's not because we are recognized authors or ministers; in fact, most don't know this about us. It's because we talk to them and ask about their affairs. Some who do know what we do have asked us to pray in times of need. They light up when we come in, and many times we get extra portions or deals others don't. Again, do we honor them for the extras? No, a thousand times no. We do, because God gave us the charge to honor all.

Practical Examples

Let me give you some practical examples of honoring all. When you meet a person, look them in the eyes, address them kindly, make it known to them they are important to you. Don't just seek to fulfill your agenda, such as the order, request, purchase, etc. Rather take just a moment and ask about their affairs; if time permits, don't just ask one question, but probe and seek out what's important to them. Once a person knows you care about them, the door is now open for you to offer the greatest gift, the gospel of Jesus Christ. However, if you don't show you value them, and attempt to bring the gospel, they will often feel they're being used—another proselyte prospect for you to add to your collection.

Think of things you can do for people beyond the "expected"; give them a small gift, a tip when it is not necessary, or assistance with a task. Offer the garbage men a soda, or someone who is working on your residence some food. Shovel the snow off your neighbor's driveway; mow their lawn as a total surprise. It becomes fun to honor people, especially when it is not at all expected. These small things are what will set you apart and give them the desire to hear the message of Jesus Christ.

Again, what's most important is that you ask God to put true honor in your heart for all people. If you try to honor without it residing in your heart, it will come out fake, or at best shallow. It will actually have the opposite effect of what you hope. Insincerity is not hard to spot; most can sense it. At the close of the final chapter we will pray together and ask God to place true honor in our hearts. The word of God in this book has been building your faith and hunger for it; all we'll have to do is ask. Before we do, there is one final important point to cover.

CHAPTER 17

Honoring God

∝

Last, but not least—and in reality, first in importance—the only way to walk in true honor is to first and foremost always honor God. Enduring honor is found only in valuing Him above anything or anyone else. Proverbs 3:9 commands us to, "Honor the LORD."

We are to value, esteem, respect, and reverence Him above anyone or anything. We dishonor Him if we value anyone or anything above Him. He is the Great King; He is worthy to receive all our respect, not just a portion. To God alone does our honor transcend to worship.

Remember, the ultimate goal is to honor God. Our honor toward authorities, those on our level, and the "little ones" passes to Jesus, and ultimately to the Father. So when honoring people supersedes honoring and obeying God, it falls under the label of fading honor or idolatry, rather than enduring honor.

Fading Honor

Eli was head priest. He was given charge over the tabernacle during the days of Samuel's childhood. His sons were scoundrels who had no respect for the Lord, His people, or their duties as priests. They would take the best of the offerings for themselves, and if the worshipers complained they would take it by force.

Eli was aware of his sons' treacherous behavior with the offerings, along with their seducing the young women who served at the entrance of the tabernacle. Eventually he corrected them by saying, "I have been hearing reports from the people about the wicked things you are doing. Why do you keep sinning? You must stop, my sons! The reports I hear among the LORD's people are not good" (1 Sam. 2:23–24, NLT). Even though he confronted them, he continued to allow his sons to serve as priests. There was a benefit for Eli; his gluttonous eating habits were being satisfied by his sons' behavior. If he really honored God, he would have removed them from office. He would have replaced them with righteous men who would serve God and the people with true hearts. Now hear the word of the Lord that came to Eli from a prophet:

> One day a prophet came to Eli and gave him this message from the LORD: "Didn't I reveal myself to your ancestors when the people of Israel were slaves in Egypt? I chose your ancestor Aaron from among all his relatives to be my priest, to offer sacrifices on my altar, to burn incense, and to wear the priestly garments as he served me. And I assigned the sacrificial offerings to you priests. So why do you scorn my sacrifices and offerings? Why do you *honor* your sons more than me—for you and they have become fat from the best offerings of my people!"
>
> —1 Sam. 2:27–29 (NLT, emphasis mine)

The prophet nailed Eli's motives; he preferred the benefit of the best offerings taken by manipulation and force to integrity. God, through the prophet, stated that Eli *honored* his sons more than God. In doing so he would not only receive no reward, but rather the opposite—great loss. For hear what God goes on to say through the prophet:

"Therefore, the LORD, the God of Israel, says: The terrible things you are doing cannot continue! I had promised that your branch of the tribe of Levi would always be my priests. But I will honor only those who honor me, and I will despise those who despise me. I will put an end to your family, so it will no longer serve as my priests. All the members of your family will die before their time. None will live to a ripe old age. You will watch with envy as I pour out prosperity on the people of Israel. But no members of your family will ever live out their days. Those who are left alive will live in sadness and grief, and their children will die a violent death. And to prove that what I have said will come true, I will cause your two sons, Hophni and Phinehas, to die on the same day! Then I will raise up a faithful priest who will serve me and do what I tell him to do. I will bless his descendants, and his family will be priests to my anointed kings forever. Then all of your descendants will bow before his descendants, begging for money and food. 'Please,' they will say, 'give us jobs among the priests so we will have enough to eat.'"

—1 Sam. 2:30–36 (NLT)

God said He would raise up a faithful priest who would obey God over pleasing himself or people. This is true honor. The reward for this priest who would replace Eli was that he and his descendants would never lose their place, and they would have abundance of blessing.

Abraham's Honor

Abraham honored God in this manner. No one was more important to him than Isaac. He'd waited for his promised son for twenty-five years. He loved him more than anything or anyone else. Yet, one night God came to him and requested Abraham honor Him over his son. God asked him to put Isaac to death. Can you imagine the turmoil in Abraham's soul? Nothing could have been asked of him that was more difficult to give up. It would have been easier to relinquish all of his possessions than to give up the one through whom his posterity would come. Yet, we see just the opposite with Abraham as we saw with Eli. We read, "The next morning Abraham got up early" (Gen. 22:3, NLT). He didn't hesitate; he was on his way early the next morning to do what God commanded him to do.

Abraham honored God more than anything else. For this reason, just prior to him putting Isaac to death, the angel called out to him, "Do not hurt the boy in any way, for now I know that you truly fear God. You have not withheld even your beloved son from me" (v. 12, NLT). To reiterate, all true honor is a by-product of holy fear. Now hear the reward Abraham received from his act of supreme honor:

> Then the angel of the LORD called again to Abraham from heaven, "This is what the LORD says: Because you have obeyed me and have not withheld even your beloved son, I swear by my own self that I will bless you richly. I will multiply your descendants into countless millions, like the stars of the sky and the sand on the seashore. They will conquer their enemies, and through your descendants, all the nations of the earth will be blessed—all because you have obeyed me."
>
> —Gen. 22:15–18 (NLT)

Remember, honor always carries a reward, whether you honor God directly, or indirectly by honoring His servants.

Moses' Wrong Choice

Moses was another who was on the verge of losing it all because of honoring another over God. His error was severe; God was quite angry, in fact, enough so Moses' life was about to be snuffed out. We read: "On the journey, when Moses and his family had stopped for the night, the LORD confronted Moses and was about to kill him" (Ex. 4:24, NLT).

Before discussing this, let me first set up what's taking place. The Lord had just appeared to him at the burning bush. God announced He'd chosen Moses to deliver all Israel from Egypt. Moses came down from the mountain, gathered his wife and children, and started on the journey to Egypt to fulfill what he was told to do. The first night they camped God came to kill Moses. What? Kill the one He just told would deliver His people? Is God schizophrenic? No, a thousand times, no! What is going on here?

When Moses came down from the mountain after the burning-bush encounter, his wife was one of the first to meet with him. She could see Moses had experienced something profound and inquired about it. I can see their conversation going something like this:

"Sweetheart!" exclaims Moses. "God appeared to me and told me I am to go back to Egypt and deliver my people from Pharaoh's bondage. So basically, I'm the deliverer we've long been talking about."

His wife, Zipporah, responds, "Amazing, I'm with you, babe. When do we leave?"

Moses replies, "Immediately, but we have to do one thing first. On the mountain God reviewed with me the covenant He made with Abraham. He told me we are to circumcise our two boys."

She responds, "Oh, well, all right, let's start with Gershom, our oldest."

Zipporah then watches Moses perform the circumcision.

Now let's break here and allow me to say this. I witnessed our third son's circumcision. The doctor warned us to brace ourselves before the procedure. He said we'd never again see Alec in such pain. When the doctor clamped down and made the cut, I saw every fiber of Alec's being scream out. I was in agony watching him in such pain.

Let's apply this to Zipporah. She watches as her oldest son screams, wails, and writhes in pain. It most likely horrifies her. How can her husband do this to their beloved son? She's wondering about the man she's married. What happened to him on that mountain? Could this God he'd met be this bloody and cruel?

So Mom steps in. She comes between Moses and their youngest son, Eliezer; hands on hips, feet planted, and boldly postured in protest. She is in no uncertain terms communicating, *Don't take one step closer*. She protests, "You aren't doing that again. This is my baby; it's bad enough I had to witness you doing this cruel and unjust torturous act to Gershom. What kind of husband are you!"

I can only imagine the immense marriage feud that erupted. She argues, then yells, and possibly even threatens Moses. The fight goes on the entire day, through the night, and into the next day. No meals are being made, and the threats are getting worse by the hour. To Moses it seems endless, and it is wearing on him.

Finally, Moses gets fed up with the resistance of his wife, so he thinks, *I'm tired of fighting, I've got a job to do, I have a call on my life to deliver an entire nation, and I've got to get started.* So he gives in and says, "Okay, let's just go."

On their way to Egypt, the Lord comes to their camp to kill Moses, because he honored his wife over honoring God. God will not have it with His chosen leader. He will kill Moses and find another. However, once Moses wife sees what is about to happen to her husband, she gets smart and circumcises her son. We read, "[Now apparently he had failed to circumcise one of his sons, his wife being opposed to it; but seeing his life in such danger] Zipporah took a flint knife and cut off the foreskin of her son and cast it to touch Moses' feet, and said, Surely a husband of blood you are to me!" (Ex. 4:25, AMP).

Once she did this, "the LORD left him alone" (v. 26, NLT). One day in prayer God questioned me, "Did I come to kill Moses, or did I come to kill his wife?"

I soberly responded, "Moses."

God then said to me, "Yes, because I told Moses to circumcise his sons, he was the head of the household, and he chose to honor his wife's demands over Mine. He was responsible." That showed me the importance of not compromising truth in order to please those under our authority.

Moses was acting as a *peacekeeper*, instead of a *peacemaker*. Jesus never said, "Blessed are the *peacekeepers*" (see Matt. 5:9), rather, "Blessed are the *peacemakers*." A *peacekeeper* is one who will compromise truth in order to maintain a false sense of peace. Leaders can easily fall into this trap. This in essence is honoring the one we see over the One we don't see. God loathes this behavior.

A *peacemaker*, on the other hand, is one who confronts, if need be to have true peace. For this reason Jesus says, "And from the days of John the Baptist until the present time, the kingdom of heaven has endured violent assault, and violent men seize it by force [as a precious prize—a share in the heavenly kingdom is sought with most ardent zeal and intense exertion]" (Matt. 11:12, AMP). The kingdom of God is *peace* (see Rom. 14:17), and in order to have true peace we at times must be confrontational.

Selfish interests usually motivate *peacekeepers*. They don't want to make life uncomfortable for themselves, or they like the benefit they're receiving from those they should confront, such as Eli did with his sons.

Moses most likely learned from this incident, and would never compromise truth again to honor someone else's request. So in essence, this failure in the beginning of his ministry became a marker for him, a point of learning, the place a firm conviction became established within his heart that would make him a great leader the rest of his life. Eli was different. He wasn't as new and fresh in leadership as Moses, but a seasoned veteran. He knew exactly what he was doing. Moses, on the other hand, was probably just trying to be a good husband. He was sincere, but sincerely wrong.

Household Challenge

If you examine all the incidents I've illustrated in this chapter you'll notice every example takes place within the family. Eli and Abraham in regard to children, Moses with his wife. At this point, Jesus' words in regard to households become clear:

> Do not think that I came to bring peace on the earth. I did not come to bring peace but a sword. For I have come to "set a man against his father, a daughter against her mother, and a daughter-in-law against her mother-in-law"; and "a man's enemies will be those of his own household." He who loves (*honors*) father or mother more than Me is not worthy of Me. And he who loves (*honors*) son or daughter more than Me is not worthy of Me.
>
> —Matt. 10:34–37 (words in parentheses mine)

When we compromise the will of God, as revealed in His Word, in order to honor someone, even if it's within our own family, we in essence sin against God. I hope you can see the gravity of it; Jesus' words are straightforward and stern. We can see why in our examples listed above. For Eli, there would be no escaping the pronounced judgment of his family. Honoring his sons more than God came at a very high price.

In this lies the proper balance of honor. In this entire book we've focused on the importance of honoring; however, honor given above God falls under the category of dishonor or idolatry against Him, and most often carries severe consequences. Nothing, or no one, is to be honored above Him. He is God, King, and our Savior. We must always keep this in the forefront of all we do.

Honor Is Displayed by Obedience

There are many other incidents throughout the Scriptures where men or women honored people over God. None of the outcomes are favorable. We've shown the consequences of honoring those under our authority; in regard to those who are on our level, or over us, the same is true.

One, which sobers me deeply, is found with a young and old prophet in the book of Kings. The young prophet from Judah was instructed by God to go to Bethel and cry out against the idolatrous altar, on which King Jeroboam sacrificed. He did, and God split the altar apart, and ashes poured out exactly as the young prophet spoke.

King Jeroboam was overwhelmed by how quickly the man of God's word came to pass, and the power of God that healed his hand. So the king invited the prophet to his palace to be refreshed and given a reward. To which the prophet replied: "If you were to give me half your house, I would not go in with you; nor would I eat bread nor drink water in this place. For so it was commanded me by the word of the LORD, saying, 'You shall not eat bread, nor drink water, nor return by the same way you came'" (1 Kings 13:8–9).

So he went out another way and started his journey back to Judah. However, an old prophet met him on the way and invited him to his house to eat. The young prophet again told the older prophet what God spoke to him—he wasn't to eat or drink, nor return the same way, and he couldn't go with him. However, the old prophet then spoke up: "I am a prophet, too, just as you are. And an angel gave me this message from the LORD: 'Bring him home with you, and give him food to eat and water to drink.'" But the old man was lying to him (v. 18, NLT).

The young prophet honored the words of the older prophet and went home with him. Once in the house, while eating, the word of the Lord was spoken to the young prophet that because he'd disobeyed he would not come to the grave of his ancestors.

He then left for Judah and was met by a lion on the road and killed. However, the lion did not eat his corpse, nor did he devour or eat the donkey the prophet traveled upon. When the old prophet discovered the fate of the young prophet, he said with certainty, "The LORD has delivered him to the lion, which has torn him and killed him, according to the word of the LORD which He spoke to him" (v. 26).

The young prophet respected the old prophet. Most likely, this respect for elders was developed at a young age. It was a strong conviction in his being to honor men who'd been in God's service longer than he; and this is a good virtue. However, a proper balance must be maintained. The young prophet's grave error was in honoring the older prophet's words over the word of the Lord. It cost him dearly.

An example from the New Testament is found in the life of Peter. The apostle Paul records,

> When Peter came to Antioch, I had a face-to-face confrontation with him because he was clearly out of line. Here's the situation. Earlier, before certain persons had come from James, Peter regularly ate with the non-Jews. But when that conservative group came from Jerusalem, he cautiously pulled back and put as much distance as he could manage between himself and his non-Jewish friends. That's how fearful he was of the conservative Jewish clique that's been pushing the old system of circumcision. Unfortunately, the rest of the Jews in the Antioch church joined in that hypocrisy so that even Barnabas was swept along in the charade.
>
> Galatians 2:11–13 (The Message)

Why did Peter, Barnabas, and the other Jewish believers pull back from the non-Jewish believers when they freely ate with them earlier? The answer is simple—they honored their friends above truth, and this resulted in fearful and hypocritical behavior. Peter knew the truth; it had been revealed to him in a trance while in Joppa.

The exact word of the Lord to him was, "Do not consider anything unclean that God has declared clean" (Acts 10:15, TEV).

Again, I'm aware sometimes it's easier to honor the one we face than the One we cannot see. However, this must not be so. We must set boundaries of convictions in our lives to regulate our responses. So if one we respect or love asks, entices, or tries to persuade us to go against what we know to be the word of God, we cannot honor their wishes above God's.

Withholding Honor

There are times to withhold honor. Though rare, it must be addressed so we don't fall into sin. We read,

> Like snow in the summer and like rain in harvest, so honor is not fitting for a [self-confident] fool.
>
> —Proverbs 26:1 (AMP)

> Honoring a fool is as foolish as tying a stone to a slingshot.
>
> —Proverbs 26:8 (NLT)

To tie a stone to a slingshot will result in no one getting injured but you. How does this apply to everyday life? First, who is the fool? He is the one who says in his heart there is no God (see Ps. 53:1); spreads slander (see Prov. 10:18); does evil like a sport (see Prov. 10:23); is always right in his own eyes and does not seek godly counsel (see Prov. 12:15); speaks pompous and proud words (see Prov. 14:3); is self-confident and despises wisdom, knowledge, and correction (see Prov. 15:5; 18:2)—just to name a few of the traits assigned to a fool in Scripture. In short, a person such as this is often referred to as an antichrist in the New Testament, because they live completely contrary to the ways and teachings of Jesus Christ.

When we honor such a person for his or her folly, we bring harm to ourselves; the stone of our slingshot strikes us back. The apostle John makes this quite clear in his second epistle:

> If anyone comes to you and does not bring this doctrine [is disloyal to what Jesus Christ taught], do not receive him [do not accept him, do not welcome or admit him] into [your] house or bid him Godspeed *or* give him any encouragement. For he who wishes him success [who encourages him, wishing him Godspeed] is a partaker in his evil doings.
>
> —2 John 10–11 (AMP)

It is unwise to honor dishonorable behavior or beliefs contrary to the doctrine of Christ. If we do, we become partaker of their sin.

Obtaining Honor

Finally, as stated earlier, it is contrary to the heart of God to demand honor. If a husband hears a message on honor but returns home and demands it from his wife and children, he misses the gist of the message. It would be the same for any other in a position of authority. On the other hand, Scripture teaches what we can do to attract honor to our lives:

> Get wisdom! Get understanding! Do not forget, nor turn away from the words of my mouth. Do not forsake her, and she will preserve you; love her, and she will keep you. Wisdom *is* the principal thing; therefore get wisdom. And in all your getting, get understanding. Exalt her, and she will promote you; she will **bring you honor, when you embrace her.**
>
> —Proverbs 4:5–8 (emphasis mine)

Embracing wisdom will bring you honor. The starting place of wisdom is the fear of the Lord. When we fear the Lord we'll believe and obey the Word of God in all areas of our lives. We desire to always obey all His commands and precepts. I find there are people who try to make the Scriptures fit into their lifestyle or beliefs. Therefore when they read the Bible, they end up *reading what they believe*, instead of *believing what they read*. The former is deceit; the latter is the fear of the Lord, which leads to wisdom.

People who strive to live justly, love mercy, and walk humbly before God are those who are quick to repent and believe. They are those who will accept correction when needed. We are told, "Poverty and shame will come to him who disdains correction, but he who regards a rebuke will be honored" (Prov. 13:18). The opposite of shame is honor. Resist correction, and you'll invite dishonor; but to love truth more than personal comfort or pleasure, will draw honor.

It simply comes down to this: "By humility and the fear of the LORD are riches and honor and life" (Prov. 22:4). God promises honor if you pursue godliness. It may not come immediately, but it always will come. Now that I've been in ministry for decades, I've observed those who walk in the enduring blessings of God. With some, for a season it appeared as if their faithfulness would not be rewarded; however, through steadfast patience they eventually see great honor and blessing.

Retaining Honor

To retain honor we must stay humble in spirit. No matter how abundantly God blesses us, we must always remember, there is nothing we have we weren't given. When Lisa and I started in traveling ministry we didn't have much, nor were we sought out. We purposed to give our all to whatever doors God opened for us. After years of seeing our needs met many times in the eleventh hour, God spoke to me in prayer: "Son, I'm going to begin to bless you, your family, and your ministry in a way that is beyond your dreams. You will have abundant provision, and the influence of your ministry will become much greater. However, it will also be a test for you. In the dry times you've trusted me for everything; what you should speak, how you should spend money, where you should go, and so forth. When I bless you abundantly, will you start to give your opinions, or continue to look to Me for what to say; will you just spend money anywhere, or still seek My counsel; will you no longer look to Me for where to go and what to do; will you forget where you've come from?"

Then He said, "Son, most who've fallen, did so in the abundant times, not the dry times."

I remember walking home (I had been out in a remote place near our house) and telling my wife what God spoke to me in prayer. She soberly looked at me and said, "John, had you told me just the first part, that God was going to abundantly bless us, I would have been dancing right now; but in hearing the warning, holy fear has overwhelmed me."

I nodded in agreement.

Paul, for his entire life, referred to himself as the "least of the apostles," "least of all the saints," and "chief of sinners." He never forgot where he came from and this eternal truth: that what he had, God gave him. For this reason he wrote, "For who makes you differ from another? And what do you have that you did not receive?" (1 Cor. 4:7). When we live humbly before God in this manner, we will not lose what we've labored for. Recall the verse of Scripture we opened the book with: "Look to yourselves, that we do not lose those things we worked for, but that we may receive a full reward" (2 John 8). To keep us from losing the fruit of our labor, we are exhorted,

"A man's pride will bring him low, but the humble in spirit will *retain* honor."

—Prov. 29:23 (emphasis mine)

Notice the word *retain*. We will maintain, as well as grow in, honor if live in the fear of the Lord and walk in true humility. Never forget how great a death Jesus delivered you from. Also remember His love and the value of every individual you come in contact with is just as great. So honor them, as He honored them by giving His life, and you will gain honor, receive rewards, and retain what you've received.

Conclusion

Repeatedly we've emphasized that all true honor comes from the heart. One of the most effective ways our heart is changed is through genuine prayer. I encourage you to pray daily for God's love, holy fear, and honor to abound in your heart. So to close this book but not close the message in your heart, for it will continue to bear fruit in your life—I want to pray with you for God to pour into your being genuine honor for those He brings into your life. If you've neglected to honor some, I begin the prayer with repentance. Let's pray together:

Father in heaven, thank You for speaking to me through this book. I come before You and first of all ask Your forgiveness. Please forgive me for neglecting to honor those You've sent into my life. For not respecting and submitting to those who are over me in authority; as well as not honoring those on my level; along with not valuing those who are under my entrusted authority; and finally for not honoring all men and women with whom I've come in contact. I ask You to cleanse me with the blood of Jesus, for I repent of my insensitivity toward certain individuals.

I ask that You would immerse my heart and soul with true honor. I desire the fear of the Lord and divine love to be shed abroad in my heart. I'm asking You cause my heart to burn, as Your Heart yearns, in seeing men and women valued, loved, respected, and honored. I ask this in faith and receive it at this time; and it's in Jesus' name I pray, Amen.

Again, pray along these lines daily, walk in obedience to the Word of God, and watch yourself transformed into being a greater ambassador of the kingdom of God. Your reward will be great, and you will experience joy and fulfillment of heart. Thank you for your love and service to our King.

Now to Him who is able to keep you from stumbling, and to present you faultless before the presence of His glory with exceeding joy, to God our Savior, Who alone is wise, be glory and majesty, dominion and power, both now and forever. Amen.

—Jude 1:24–25

About the Author

❧

JOHN BEVERE is passionate to see individuals deepen their intimacy with God and experience a rewarding life both now and for eternity. He is the author of such bestsellers as *The Bait of Satan*, *The Fear of the Lord*, *Under Cover*, and *Driven by Eternity*. His books have been translated into forty-eight languages and his weekly television program, *The Messenger*, is broadcast around the world. He is a popular speaker at conferences and churches, and his ministry, Messenger International, offers resources to those who want to understand God's principles. John's wife, Lisa, is also a bestselling author and speaker. They reside with their family in Colorado Springs, Colorado.

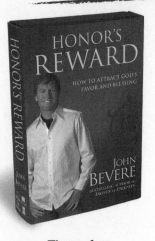

BOOKS BY JOHN

The Bait of Satan

Breaking Intimidation

The Devil's Door

Drawing Near

Driven by Eternity

The Fear of the Lord

A Heart Ablaze

Honor's Reward

How to Respond when you Feel Mistreated

Rescued

Thus Saith the Lord

Under Cover

Victory in the Wilderness

Voice of One Crying

Rescued - Audio Theater
2 hours on 2 CDs

Starring:
Roma Downey from *Touched by an Angel*
John Rhys-Davies from *The Lord of the Rings*
Marisol Nichols from the hit TV show *24*

**From the
novel
Rescued**

A trapped father. A desperate son. A clock ticking down toward certain death and a fate even more horrible still...

For Alan Rockaway, his teenaged son Jeff, and new bride Jenny, it's been little more than a leisurely end to a weeklong cruise ...a horrifying crash and even more, a plunge toward the unknown...

Everything Alan has assumed about himself is flipped upside down. In the ultimate rescue operation, life or death is just the beginning!

Driven by Eternity - curriculum

We have taken this powerful message, *Driven by Eternity*, and created an individual kit and small group upgrade for further, in-depth study. You can now share this life-transforming message with friends and family through bible studies, small groups, and church services.

INCLUDED IN THE INDIVIDUAL CURRICULUM:

- 12 - 40 MINUTE LESSONS ON 4 DVD'S
- DRIVEN BY ETERNITY HARDBACK BOOK
- HARDBACK DEVOTIONAL WORKBOOK

GET THE 4-CD
AUDIO DRAMA
AFFABEL
FREE
WITH PURCHASE

Affabel - Audio Theater
2.5 hours on 4 CDs

FEATURING JOHN RHYS-DAVIES
AND A CAST OF HOLLYWOOD ACTORS

AN EPIC AUDIO DRAMA PORTRAYING THE REALITY OF THE JUDGMENT SEAT OF CHRIST— GET READY TO BE CHANGED FOREVER... AND PREPARE FOR ETERNITY!

Packaging subject to change.

This audio dramatization, taken from John Bevere's book *Driven by Eternity*, will capture your heart and soul as you experience life on "the other side" where eternity is brought into the present and all must stand before the Great King and Judge. Be prepared for a roller coaster ride of joy, sorrow, astonishment, and revelation as lifelong rewards are bestowed on some while others are bound hand and foot and cast into outer darkness by the Royal Guard!